D1550871

I Didn't
Place
in the
Talent
Race
but...

I Didn't Place in the Talent Race but...

Anya Bateman

Deseret Book Company
Salt Lake City, Utah

Library of Congress Cataloging-in-Publication Data

Bateman, Anya.
   I didn't place in the talent race, but— : a woman's guide to
recognizing her strengths / by Anya Bateman.
      p.   cm.
   Includes index.
   ISBN 0-87579-354-1
      1. Women, Mormon—Religious life.   2. Self-respect—Religious
aspect—Christianity.   I. Title.
BX8641.B32   1990
248.8'43—dc20
                                                        90-36186
                                                           CIP

Printed in the United States of America
10   9   8   7   6   5   4   3   2   1

Contents

Introduction

How difficult it is to see our own strengths, talents, or gifts! I hadn't really paid much attention to this common problem until my friend Lee Ann telephoned me some time ago. This woman is amazingly articulate. She can express herself beautifully and eloquently in all situations. Words just flow from her lips as if she's hooked up to a heavenly tape recorder.

I had admired her ability for quite a while, and on that particular day I decided it was time I mentioned it. Her reaction took me by surprise. "Oh, no, no!" she objected. "That just isn't true at all. You're talking about one of my worst areas!"

Realizing that we sometimes feel a need to act humble when our strengths are mentioned, I pursued. I was sure that with such high degree of talent, she simply had to be aware of it. How could she *not* be aware of it, when it was so obvious to the rest of us?

But again she disclaimed her gift. I sensed sincerity as she said that she, of all people, had no talent in that area. Why, she couldn't put two words together properly!

I realized suddenly that when we fail to see our strengths or talents, in a very real sense we bury them. In Christ's parable

1

of the talents, the servant that we're most familiar with is the one who buried the talent he was allotted and then was chastised by his master, who had given it to him. Obviously, the servant knew exactly what he had to work with and what it was worth, and still he chose to bury it.

We often use this parable to talk about the talents we each possess. With these talents, though, the problem is sometimes a little different. Instead of knowing precisely and clearly what our allotment is, we're often confused about what our gifts and strengths really are. I have been surprised at the people who say such things as, "I wish I had something I could do well" or "You're lucky to have something you're good at." Often these are the very people I am in awe of and whose talents I recognize easily!

We seem to grossly underestimate the worth of what we have. We often don't even recognize what we have at all. Our talents are buried in the sense that we can't see them, we may not even know what we have, and we certainly don't know where they're buried.

So what does all that mean? If we don't know what our talents are, we can't use them, and it certainly is difficult to multiply them. In fact, we don't even know we're already rich. Think of the man who searched his entire life for wealth in far-off places, only to have one of the world's richest diamond mines discovered in his backyard. This man never benefited from the treasures right there for him all the time.

We fail to benefit from our treasures if we aren't aware of them and don't recognize them or know where they are. They remain buried. The really strange part is that all kinds of treasures are right there before us. All kinds of talents and strengths are waiting right there. They're available. We were meant to find them.

So how do we get to them? How do we learn to recognize our talents, gifts, abilities, and strengths? Let's look together.

Chapter 1

Without Exception

The talent program we attended had been held to honor excellence and to uplift and inspire us. Afterward, as we drove home, I didn't realize at first that Janette wasn't feeling inspired. She wasn't even feeling uplifted. "Did you notice that painting of the waterfall?" I asked. "Wasn't it incredible? I could almost feel the water on my face."

"It was beautiful, all right," my friend replied without inflection.

"And that soprano." I continued. "Her voice was positively ethereal."

"I know," Janette said miserably.

Then I caught on. "You're right," I said with a laugh. "It was all rather depressing, wasn't it."

Janette nodded and blinked. I could tell she wasn't going to joke along. "I don't even know why I go to things like that," she said. "Whenever I do, I come away wondering what I've been doing with my time and what's wrong with me. I see all those amazing talents, and I come away feeling like such a loser."

Unfortunately, Janette's feelings are not unusual. For some

reason, very few of us feel wonderful about what we've been given in the way of talents, gifts, and strengths. We feel short-changed or left out. We feel others received so much more. Oh yes, the talents and strengths of others are obvious to us. But what about our own?

It seems that not only do we feel inadequate about our gifts at times but we also fail even to recognize that we have them. We're often more aware of what's in our closets or in our checking accounts or in our food storage than we are of our other resources that can affect the very core of our lives, our purpose, the directions we take, our sense of self, and, most assuredly, our confidence and how we feel about ourselves.

Sometimes our blindness to what's good in ourselves is profound. Linda is one of the most aware women I know. Whenever I need to find out what's going on, whether in the world or in the neighborhood, I phone her. She knows where to find bargains and where to find excellence. One day while we were talking I mentioned to her how strange it seemed that some of the most talented people can't see what they have.

"Then there are people like me," said this capable woman. "We can't see our talents because there are none there to see."

"You're kidding, of course," I exclaimed.

Again I sensed sincerity as Linda spoke. "I wish I were."

I almost laughed. "But you have talents. You know very well that everyone has talents and gifts and strengths. We've talked about that."

"Oh, sure, I believe that in general, that's true," she replied. I realized that she felt she was an exception.

Perhaps the first thing we need to convince one another of, then, is that there are no exceptions to this rule. Whether we choose to believe it or not, we really do all have significant strengths, gifts, powers, abilities, and talents.

Dr. Calvin Taylor illustrated that fact through some studies he did in schools several years ago. Discouraged that conventional programs stressed only the academic talents and failed to recognize the many other talents of intelligence, he introduced a new approach in some test classrooms. The teachers, as "talent developers," were asked to help draw out other strengths in the children, gifts such as the ability to communicate, to anticipate, to make decisions. To develop a talent for planning, for instance, teachers assigned a committee of students to plan a class outing or party. To learn decision making, students were given opportunities to gather information and make logical choices. Later, when the children were tested, it was evident in each test classroom that no longer were just one or two children excelling or even a handful doing above-average work. Instead, whole classrooms full of children were showing outstanding performance in one area or another.

Dr. Taylor compared the searching for talents and strengths to mining for rich ores. The depth and breadth of what we could call "gold mines" of potential as human beings has been studied by scientists who recognize the marvelous things that could be accomplished if we learned how to tap the human resource. Several years ago I read a research paper by Dr. Herbert Otto that later became the book *Guide to Developing Your Potential* (New York: Charles Scribner's Sons, 1967). The paper helped me glimpse our power as human beings. Dr. Otto pointed out that neurological findings indicate that as we learn, the brain's cortex develops fibers in the particular learning area that is exercised. In other words, the more we use our thinking powers, the more ability we create to use them. It's true that in our culture we generally limit formal education to the first quarter of our lives, but there is evidence, according to Dr. Otto, that were we to continue our studies and use more of our brain, we, as human beings, would be capable of learning up to forty languages and could master the requirements of dozens of colleges.

Our senses and our abilities to perceive are highly un-
derrated as well. We have at our disposal an "extraordinary
sensitivity to an extensive range of stimuli and data." In fact,
our minds record a great variety of stimuli we aren't even
aware of consciously. The acutely developed senses of primitive
peoples is evidence of what we are capable of. Native Americans
could actually tell the size and weight and age of a deer just
by looking at its tracks. Changes in weather were often accurately predicted by medicine men even when there were no
indications of change. Frontiersmen, who were at first aston-
ished at such abilities and powers, were less surprised later
when they themselves developed the same sensitivities and
skills in order to survive.

It occurs to me that the woman who becomes a mother
has exactly the same kind of experience. She, too, in order to
survive and help her children do likewise, finds resources
within herself, more keen senses, and skills she didn't know
she had. I marveled at my own mother's ability always to know
exactly what I was doing. Why, she could hear the rustle of a
candy wrapper at a three-room distance! Now my own children
are in awe of my super senses. I've even convinced them that
I can read it in their eyes if they're telling fibs. And, frankly, I
generally can.

Dr. Otto cited as additional evidence of our human potential the intense growing and learning that take place in early
childhood. Children are highly aware of things around them,
and they live in the moment and with the moment, excited
and alive—the epitome of living at full potential.

Dr. Otto also pointed out that when it comes to creativity,
our society has done poorly at taking advantage of the powers
we have within us, but that if creativity were to be more fully
tapped, a "cultural renaissance unequalled in history would
result."

As Latter-day Saint women, our concern may be more in

line with getting through the day than creating a cultural renaissance. I, for one, would like to have the power to handle twelve telephone calls in a five-minute period. We're burdened by a lack of time and an overabundance of responsibilities in our adult years. Then what good does it do to know of our potential as human beings?

Because some of the burden we often bear is the low opinion we have of ourselves, recognizing how remarkable we *all* are can lift our spirits, even before we're able to admit to the worth of our individual talents, strengths, and assets. We can feel better about ourselves when we realize that regardless of how lacking we feel personally, we cannot deny that we are remarkable, nevertheless, because of the awesome powers of our bodies and minds. As we gain appreciation for ourselves as human beings, we take a step closer to an appreciation for ourselves individually.

In a speech called "The Magnificence of Man" (*Ensign*, Jan. 1988, pp. 64–69), Elder Russell M. Nelson concurred that we are indeed remarkable. As a physician he is familiar with the miraculous design of the body's individual organs. Without cords or batteries, the eyes are connected to the brain, where sights can be recorded. The ears perceive sound, which they transmit to the brain along nerve lines. "This marvelous sound system is also connected to the recording instrument of the brain." Further, declared Elder Nelson, the human brain is a recording instrument whose magnificence is beyond our comprehension.

Elder Nelson also pointed out that the body has a powerful ability to adapt and protect and repair and renew itself. Each cell of our bodies is formed from the earth's elements according to the "recipe" or formula contained within our unique genes.

What a marvelous work and a wonder we are! What powers our physical bodies have! But even more glorious, Elder Nelson emphasized, is the wonder of the spirit. It's true. If our powers and potential seem awesome from a strictly physical perspective, then from a spiritual and eternal perspective, our potential is impossible for us to fathom. From that higher perspective, as miraculous as our minds are, their potential is so awesome that we can't imagine such power.

Through revelation we can, however, get an inkling of this incredible potential. Heavenly Father tells us in Doctrine and Covenants 82:18 that not only do we each have talent but that we can also gain more talents, "even an hundred fold."

The concept of eternal progression and the knowledge that we are the offspring and embryo of Deity indicate that our potential is limitless. As we glimpse the marvelous potential we have all been given, we realize that we need never again say, "I have little in the way of talents or strengths."

Chapter 2

All Kinds of Talents

Why, if we have so much, is it so difficult to recognize our own strengths and gifts and then value them? Could we have trouble simply because we are so close to them? It's human nature to be blinded to the value of things we're used to. When it comes to treasures right in our own backyards, maybe they've been there for so long that they just seem a part of the everyday scenery and not at all special. Familiarity makes any treasure seem less than wondrous. Yes, I think we do take our talents for granted.

It isn't at all uncommon to feel that something accessible to us must not be worth a great deal. At a fireside I attended, Dr. Victor Cline told of a young woman who came to him for counseling because she couldn't seem to get interested in any of the young men who showed an interest in her. "If he's interested in me," was her reasoning, "he must be a loser." In the same way, we may feel that our own abilities and strengths must be of very little value or not qualified to be called talents or strengths.

Feeling uncomfortable about acknowledging our talents and gifts may also play a part in our inability to recognize them.

We're fearful of bragging, even to ourselves, and thus we don't make it a point to look for our assets because, well, it just isn't done. Besides, the scriptures tell us to be humble. As a result, consciously or unconsciously, we hesitate to find good in ourselves out of fear that it is inappropriate or even unrighteous to do so.

The strengths so obvious to us in others sometimes cause us to devalue our own. We hold contests, real or imagined. One writer compared himself to Shakespeare and consequently saw little talent in himself. "Everything's already been said much better than I could say it," he commented.

In the same vein, we often feel that our gifts must win public acclaim in order to be acceptable. We feel we must place first, or second, or at least honorable mention in this imaginary talent race. We also feel our talents and strengths must be of a certain quantity or quality or variety to be of worth or to "count." And so we go to talent seminars in which beautiful talents are displayed, and we come away feeling discouraged or depressed. We forget that talents and strengths are not just those that can be performed or displayed. Granted, the kinds of talents that are quickly acclaimed are significant. Much good may be done through them, and they certainly add beauty and richness to the world—but there are other gifts as well.

At one function I attended, everyone was amazed at the beautiful singing voices, the magnificent art work, and the speech and dramatic skills. I wondered, however, if the woman who was conducting thought of herself as talented. I have learned from experience that conducting a meeting isn't as easy as she made it look. I wondered if the people who had helped organize the event recognized their strengths. And the people in the audience—many of whom did not have talents or gifts that could be performed or displayed—did they recognize that they too had strengths and talents? Were those who were performing and otherwise displaying their talents aware of the full spectrum of those gifts — and their other strengths as well?

We often think that the word *talent* can't mean just any ability or strength, only a few that quickly come to mind. But no guidebook I know of lists abilities and strengths that count or abilities and strengths that don't count. That's because they *all* count.

In the physical realm, for instance, we quickly acknowledge the natural gifts and developed abilities of speed, grace, or agility of an athlete. We marvel at the prowess of basketball players who dunk that basketball with a skill that makes playing look easy. I love to watch my own daughter dance ballet, and I am intrigued with her natural grace and flexibility, gifts she was born with but which she has also worked to develop. Her gift seems a miracle — we can't trace it to any other family members.

Yes, we're highly aware of gifts and talents we see performed on stage or in a studio or concert hall or on the screen. But those aren't the only important physical abilities. Believe me, I broadened my view immensely when, after struggling for half the day with a renegade sheet of wallpaper, I found myself totally unnerved. No matter what I did, I could not get that sheet on the wall acceptably straight. The middle seam gaped open and glue globs bulged. I was ready to scream when I called my friend Carol, who at one time had had a business called The Wallflowers. Perhaps she heard the desperation in my voice, because she came right over. I watched in awe as in no time at all she flipped the sheet into place without so much as a ripple. "How did you do that?" I asked. "You make it look so easy."

"Ah, some of us have it, and some of us don't," Carol said with a grin. I agreed. Even though experience no doubt helped, I suspected there was some truth in what she said.

"My mother, to this day, can't get a piece of contact paper into a drawer without getting wrapped up in it herself," Carol continued. "Even when I was little, I was in charge of contact paper." I pictured a mother watching in awe as her little one, her own offspring, eased a sheet of contact paper into a drawer without any problem — the same sheet she herself had just been struggling with. I could understand Carol's mother, for my own oldest daughter can have an entire mechanical project put together in the time it takes me to figure out how to get the parts out of the packaging.

When we include all physical abilities — strengths of our physical body itself, for example, and our senses and our limbs — we realize that the list could stretch into infinity.

Very real as well are the insights we call almost magical in the arts — that indefinable something in drama, literature, music, that makes it easier for us to feel, understand, and possibly even create in those areas. But insights also present themselves in other areas that may not come to mind as quickly.

One spring I telephoned to compliment the head gardener on Temple Square in Salt Lake City for his unbelievable artistry with living plants and flowers. I was connected first to the greenhouse, and I spoke to Heinz Jelitto, the person in charge there. Realizing that some of the credit should go to him as well, I congratulated him on the gorgeous blooms, the luscious robust tulips and petunias and pansies, thick with good health. "What's your secret?" I asked. "Is it all strictly scientific?"

In his German accent, he explained that it was not all scientific. Sometimes it was more "a feeling" for what was right. Good guesses. He attributed much of his good fortune with plants to this intuitive know-how that he couldn't pinpoint — an ability to sense and make correct choices when it came to plants.

In *Dandelion Wine*, Ray Bradbury described the natural artistry of a grandmother with foods:

"If asked about her cooking, Grandma would look down at her hands which some glorious instinct sent on journeys to be gloved in flour, or to plumb disencumbed turkeys, wrist deep in search of their animal souls. Her gray eyes blinked from spectacles warped by forty years of oven blasts and blinded with strewings of pepper and sage, so she sometimes flung cornstarch over steaks, amazingly tender, succulent steaks! And sometimes dropped apricot into meat loaves, cross-pollinated meats, herbs, fruits, vegetables with no prejudice, no tolerance for recipe or formula, save that at the final moment of delivery, mouths watered, blood thundered in response. Her hands then . . . were Grandma's mystery, delight, and life. She looked at them in astonishment but let them live their life the way they absolutely must live it!" (New York: Doubleday, 1957.)

Whether we choose to consider them glorious or not, we each have sensitivities that operate within us and cause this kind of magical understanding in certain areas.

"But cooking isn't a talent," one of my neighbors informed some of us after we told her how talented she is in the kitchen. "Baking bread is just baking bread." It took three of us to convince her that it is a talent, and she is talented.

There are many artistic outlets. My cousin Janie laughs about her lack of natural ability in drawing. She claims she can't even draw a stick figure and laughs as she quotes her seventh-grade teacher, who took one look at a picture Janie had brought up to her desk and said, "May I suggest, my dear, that you never pursue art. You should definitely take another direction."

Janie did take another direction and chose to focus on stronger areas, but guess what? One of her hobbies is needle work. She especially loves the counted cross-stitch and not only finds pleasure in it, but brings joy to others with her adorable and clever gifts. Her patience for detail and her eye for color make her a natural. Maybe she can't draw well, but anyone looking at her beautiful work would call her an artist. An artist, after all, is simply someone who creates or adds beauty to this world of ours. There are many ways of doing that.

My great-grandmother was a simple soul with very little formal education. She struggled with reading and writing skills, but what wonderful stories she could tell! The other grandchildren and I spent hours sitting around her as she enriched our lives with dramas she'd heard as a young woman and committed to memory. Her characters were alive and real, and their plights were our number one concern as "Oma" included delicious details. Though I've tried to relate some of these stories to my children and have even tried to write them down, I've never yet been able to capture the feeling and intensity they exuded when my great-grandmother told them. She was an artist.

Even just the ability to appreciate beautiful music, fine art, or literature, or loveliness of any kind is a strength. Kathryn Kay shares this insight in her poem "Necessary Triad" (used by permission):

> To me it's never been quite clear
> To whom the greatest joy belongs,
> To those who write or those who hear
> Or those who sing the songs.

The bright spots of our intelligences — our minds — are sometimes overlooked completely. Yet each of us has such strengths. Some things just come to us easily. Our minds seem to grasp certain formulas or techniques or skills swiftly, and we seem to put some puzzles together even before we've been given all the pieces.

Elouise Bell cited the importance of "reserving judgment in scholastic matters," as an important humanizing lesson she has learned in her years of teaching English. In an article published in the April 1984 *BYU Today,* she told of a man who fifteen years before had come to BYU at his parents' insistence but who personally felt he was wasting his time. "You gave me C's on most of my papers," he told Sister Bell, "and there were a lot of errors, but you always said something like, 'You have some good ideas here' or 'I like your thinking.' You seemed to think I had something on the ball. I figured you must know what you were talking about so I stayed in school.' "

"Stayed in school, went on to Brandeis," continued Sister Bell, "from there to Hebrew University and a Ph.D. Now doing work on Coptic scrolls."

As Dr. Taylor discovered in school classrooms, intelligence talents are not just limited to ease in academic subjects. Children with the ability to reproduce information are definitely talented, but Dr. Taylor mined for others' talents and found them in abundance. Among them were wisdom, or common sense, and communication—talents we recognize as highly important.

Although there are no doubt others, there is one more area I'll mention that is also often overlooked: abilities of personality and character—those strengths of the spirit that are very real powers and that we also need to recognize and definitely need to count.

Janie, my cousin, may not have the ability to draw stick figures, but she does have the ability to draw out real people and make them feel comfortable. We feel we can be ourselves around Janie, say what we think, and even act a little silly, if we feel so inclined. Is her ability to draw out people less significant than the ability to draw people on paper? Of course not.

My father-in-law attracts people as if he's magnetized in some magical way. He's naturally friendly and caring, and consequently people cross gymnasiums to visit with him. They sense his affability and love of others. I'd call him talented.

A neighbor of mine generates hysteria with just the lift of

an eyebrow. She's not a professional stand-up comedienne, but she adds much light-hearted fun to everyday life — she helps us take ourselves less seriously and put our problems in perspective. She has the ability to see life through humor-colored glasses, a view she shares with others. How talented she is!

Sister Bell also told about a student in one of her classes who was mediocre in English but who invited Sister Bell to visit her where she worked. There, in the American Fork Training School, Sister Bell saw another side of this student. She saw her patience, compassion, and strength with the less fortunate: "Today, when I look at some quiet, average, student sitting in the back of my classroom, I remind myself that neither he, nor certainly I, know where his unique human spirit will take him," Sister Bell concluded.

My friend Linda, who claims she has no talents, is amazingly patient with young children. She seems to have a calming effect on them, yet she sparks their imaginations and helps them delight in life at the same time. She is also resourceful, thrifty, practical, alert, mechanically inclined, versatile, but best of all, a wonderful friend and listener, available, compassionate, and a great counselor. Perhaps Linda's talents can't be performed or framed, but they are clearly significant.

To get an idea of all the strengths that are left out when we do not include personality and character, I've listed some of the abilities that I've seen in family members and friends and some that I've come up with after searching through a dictionary and a thesaurus.

accepting	altruistic	assertive
accommodating	amenable	assiduous
adaptable	ambitious	attentive
adventuresome	amiable	believing
aggressive	amicable	benevolent
agreeable	amusing	bold
alacritous	analytical	brave
alert	ardent	bright

broadminded
calm
candid
carefree
careful
caring
casual
charismatic
cheerful
clear-thinking
clever
commanding
compassionate
confident
conscientious
conservative
considerate
consistent
content
controlled
cooperative
creative
credible
courageous
courteous
decisive
dedicated
deliberate
demonstrative
dependable
determined
devoted
dignified
diligent
diplomatic
disciplined
discreet
discriminating
distinguished
docile
down-to-earth
dramatic
droll

dry-witted
dynamic
easy-going
economical
effervescent
efficacious
efficient
elegant
eloquent
empathetic
energetic
enthusiastic
exuberant
fair
faithful
fastidious
fearless
feminine
forceful
forgiving
forthright
friendly
fun-loving
funny
gallant
generous
gentle
genuine
giving
good-natured
gracious
guileless
handy
happy
hearty
helpful
honest
honorable
hopeful
hospitable
humble
humorous
imaginative

impish
impulsive
independent
industrious
influential
inquisitive
inspiring
intelligent
interested
inventive
joking
jolly
judicious
just
keen-minded
kindhearted
kindly
level-headed
light-hearted
likeable
lively
loving
loyal
magnetic
merry
methodical
meticulous
mischievous
mild-mannered
modest
moral
natural
neat
nice
patient
peace-loving
perceptive
persevering
playful
pleasant
positive
powerful
practical

prompt
queenly
quick
quick-thinking
quiet
rational
realistic
reasonable
refined
reflective
regal
relaxed
reliable
reserved
resourceful
respectful
responsible
reverent
romantic

self-reliant
sensitive
sentimental
spiritual
steady
striving
strong
studious
supportive
tactful
talkative
teachable
temperate
thoughtful
thrifty
tolerant
tranquil
trusting
trustworthy

truthful
uncomplaining
unconventional
understanding
unselfish
valiant
versatile
vigorous
virtuous
vivacious
warm
well-balanced
whimsical
willing
wise
witty
yielding
youthful
zestful

Spiritual gifts are closely related to gifts of character. The Doctrine and Covenants speaks of specific spiritual gifts, and it's not difficult to see them shining in our souls. Some of us have natural strengths of spirit in one area. Others have natural strengths in other areas.

For one woman, faith might come naturally and without much effort: "I've never had any trouble believing completely," she says.

For another, mercy and the ability to make peace are a real and priceless gift.

For still another, honesty is such a natural part of her makeup that she has problems telling even little white lies.

Sisters in general seem to have been endowed with a natural ability to feel compassion, possibly because of their tendency toward gentleness and nurturing. A woman first introduces us to the word *compassion* in the Bible. The heart of Pharoah's daughter was softened, and she "had compassion" on the baby Moses, floating in his small ark along the river's edge. (Exodus 2:6.)

So, even if we are talented in other ways, we can see that it is vitally important to acknowledge our qualities of character and our specific spiritual gifts, which are of infinite value. Then, as we look over the vast array of strengths and talents that "count," surely we can see that we can lengthen the list of our own abilities. And we will know more clearly within ourselves that the talents and strengths we hadn't counted are the very ones that count the most.

Chapter 3

Profile: Unique

"You're unique!" we're told throughout our lives. We're compared to snowflakes to remind us that no two of us are the same. In fact, at a young women's program I visited, one of the sisters in the ward had crocheted individual "snowflakes" for each of the girls. I hope the girls appreciated those elegant doilies (and I hope that devoted sister appreciated herself as well) but I wonder if the message registered fully. We've *heard* about our personal uniqueness, but do we believe it?

A fellow writer told me how dumbfounded she was when she first realized that everyone else did not feel the same passion to put things on paper that she did and that some people don't even like to write. She had assumed that creative writing was something that everyone does naturally without any problem—perhaps like eating. When she finally realized that all people don't find delight in expressing themselves on paper, she began seeing this ability in a different light.

The same can be said for every talent. The woman who speaks with eloquence may feel that everyone has the same degree of ability and does not realize the extent to which some people struggle with expressing themselves. The woman with great faith might think that faith comes naturally for everyone. When we recognize that we aren't all the same, we place greater value on what we have and are more inclined to see its worth.

Even people in the same family sometimes differ drastically in their individual talents. Alice and Jan (not their real names), for instance, are sisters who look so much alike that they are often mistaken for each other. Yet how completely different they are in their abilities and powers. Here are brief talent profiles or listings of their main talent areas:

ALICE	JAN
Leans heavily toward literature and the fine arts	Athletic with emphasis on marathon walking and basketball
Is highly creative and enjoys drawing, writing, speaking	Friendly, outgoing, and people-oriented
Has a good sense of humor	Is inclined to mathematics
Makes decisions quickly and effectively	Has a good business sense
Is dynamic	Enjoys photography
Has a flair for the unconventional and dramatic	Is an excellent seamstress
Is impulsive	Has a great sense of humor
Is intellectual	Is self-disciplined and organized
Has good self-confidence	Is sensitive
	Is guileless

It is evident that Alice leans much more heavily toward the arts. She has a number of the talents that would fit right into one of those talent programs beautifully. In fact, she could probably put one on by herself.

Jan, on the other hand, leans heavily toward academics in mathematics and business and always did well in her school subjects because of her high degree of self-discipline and ability to organize her time. She's athletic and fun-loving but much more conservative than her sister. Her artistic outlets of photography and sewing are less conventional than the quickly acclaimed talents of her sister. But it is obvious that both women are talented.

It's true that there are siblings whose gifts overlap to a much greater extent than these two sisters' gifts do. Sometimes people in our families, our friends, our neighbors, or our sisters in the gospel have talents similar to ours. Does having over-lapping talents threaten our personal uniqueness? No, not at all.

This realization hit me hard when I drew up for other people talent profiles like those I did for Alice and Jan. I had drawn up only twenty or twenty-five profiles when I realized that even if I drew up thousands of them, no two would be alike. That's because no two of us have the same combinations of talents and strengths.

Recognizing that fact can help us realize that we needn't pine over others' strengths and talents or be discouraged by what others have. We simply do not have the same raw materials and resources to work with. "To some is given one and to some another," the scriptures tell us. (D&C 46:12.) Nor do we need to allow others' treasures to blind us to our own because they are not and can never be like our treasury of gifts. We can feel completely secure in knowing that our treasures or talents and strengths combine in a wonderful way completely right for us. We have our own personal talent packages—a package no one else has.

Further, even those individual talents and strengths that appear to be the same on different profiles become changed when they are combined with the other talents and strengths on our individual profiles. How different we can be, even in those talents we supposedly have in common.

Two women for whom I'd listed leadership as a strength, for instance, are entirely different in the way they lead. One, who has the additional strengths of enthusiasm and a keen sense of humor, leads with gusto. We laugh as we follow and enjoy her. Another leader, who has deep empathy, foresight, and wisdom, handles her callings quietly and sensitively. She seems to perceive questions and problems before they arise and leads in a powerful yet loving way.

Alice and Jan are both humorous. Yet again, other strengths individualize that humor. Alice's humor is as unconventional and creative as she is. We never have any idea what Alice will say or do. Jan's humor, on the other hand, takes form in a cheerful, up-front kidding that blends in with her sensitivity and love of people. Her humor is used primarily to put people at ease.

In a writing class I taught, I asked fourteen adults to prepare an essay about mealtime. To my delight, I received fourteen entirely different papers. One essay dealt primarily with the foods aspect of the meal—the menu; another dealt with the setting of the table; another showed the dinner experience from the viewpoint of a toddler. Tone and approach differed dramatically. It was fascinating to see how different the same assignment became when it interconnected with the individual strengths and talents of fourteen different writers.

Obviously the students' interests played a part in what they decided to write about. Not only are we unique in the abilities we have but we are unique in our interests, likes, and dislikes. In fact, interests—what we get excited about—can be defined as strengths as well, for they can be positive forces in our lives.

Maybe that's why Norman Vincent Peale suggested that to find focus in our lives, we ask ourselves not only "What do I do well?" but "What gives me satisfaction?" and "What do I want?"

We can ask ourselves these same questions to help us determine who we are and how we are unique. What we can find is that our likes and interests are very closely connected to what we do well or can eventually do well.

When I finally got hold of Peter Lassig, the head gardener on Temple Square, I asked him when he had first noticed his talent. "It wasn't so much a talent back then as a love at first sight," he said. "I was working on a merit badge that involved planting a garden when my heart began to pitter pat. I recognized instantly that I could get excited about gardening."

I have neighbors who feel the same way about their own flowers and gardens, although they haven't pursued gardening as a career. "I can't wait to get up in the morning, just so I can start digging out there," says one. Maybe that's why her yard is virtually blooming with color and is such a pleasure to look at.

My expert in the wallpapering department claims she could get high on the smell of new wallpaper. A designer I read about said that even as a child he loved to run his hand across fine fabric and touch it to his face. I caught a friend doing the same thing in her sewing room as she prepared to cut into some cloth.

"I love to shop in office supply stores, and I like everything associated with business — even pencils," another friend once said. Several years later, is it any wonder she's zeroed in on business as a career?

"Each of us," said Richard Bolles, author of *What Color Is Your Parachute?* (Berkeley, Calif.: Ten Speed Press, 1989), "has unique tropisms that we know we feel instinctively drawn toward. Despite years of research, the most efficient way to predict vocational choice is simply to ask the person what he wants."

A "tropism," according to Mr. Bolles, is a biological term meaning a natural leaning toward or away from something. We could also refer to our leanings as inner drumbeats, which Thoreau implied when he said that each of us marches to a different drummer. We could say that those leanings are like the pulse under the surface indicating the thumpity-thumping of our heartbeats, telling us where our rich potential may lie.

Happily, recognizing our interests and what we enjoy does not seem to be the problem that admitting to strengths or talents seems to be. Several years ago when I asked a group of Relief Society sisters to list their talents, not one used her pencil or pen. Three-by-five cards remained blank. When I changed the wording, however, and asked them to write down the things they enjoyed, oh that was different! Pens immediately began to click.

Sometimes, it's true, we think we can no longer hear or feel who we really are because of other poundings that compete. A few years ago, my six-year-old didn't feel she knew what toy she wanted to play with. I suggested that she play "eenie meenie miney moe."

She did exactly that, but then, as her little forefinger pointed to one of the toys, she gave me a peculiar look.

"What's the matter? Don't you want to play with that one?"

"Uh uh," she said. "I wanted to play with this one." She had known all along but just hadn't realized that she knew.

In the same way, even when we think we don't feel our preferences and deep-seated leanings, when we really stop to feel and listen to that beat inside, it is there for us.

It's not so much the "eenie meenies" as the "mineys," however, that can create the greatest competing poundings and dim our ability to sense our unique inner beat and our knowledge of where we should focus our attention. Years ago I read a column by the late Sydney Harris in which he expressed his opinion about the "mineys" that sometimes confuse our thinking. He wasn't feeling very well one night, yet he chose to sit at his typewriter and work. When his wife asked him why he didn't go up to bed, he replied that tapping at his typewriter made him feel better.

Mr. Harris said then that though there might be frustrating

times in any job, doing work one enjoys is more important than money, fame, or even status. These three are uncertain, fleeting, and irksome. Satisfaction in the task or the performance itself is what remains important.

Understanding not only our aptitudes but our unique leanings can help us make choices that will lead to greater happiness in our lives. Although it is necessary to be practical, listening only to outside poundings can lead to disillusionment.

The voices of others or the crowds can also pound loudly at times, causing us to fail to hear our own inner workings. In his poem "The Road Not Taken," Robert Frost indicated that sometimes going our own direction makes "all the difference" in our lives. True, sometimes the direction others are taking may also be the right one for us. We can seek help from others, but ultimately only we can know what our own feelings are. The spirit of truth can help us tune in to who we are and where our gifts and interests lie in rich abundance.

Rosemary, a fellow English major who trudged through the tragedies of Shakespeare and plodded through the poetry of Pope, said some years after she had completed her schooling, "I finally figured out why I went into English. My sister loved it and some other friends were excited about it as well. I thought because they loved the subject, I should too. It's taken me all this time to realize that I'm not my sister or my friends. I'm me. Why did I look to others instead of myself to determine what I wanted and liked? I should have gone into home economics and music. Those are the subjects I feel drawn toward." Rosemary gradually worked her way into music and home economics and sought additional training in them, but she remembered and valued her personal uniqueness from then on.

Chapter 4

But Is It Really Okay?

At a women's conference a few years ago, Louise Roos Plummer gave a delightful talk that probably surprised many in the audience. Louise told us the fable of the grasshopper and the ant and said, "I remind you of this story so that I can tell you that even as a child it made me uncomfortable. It still makes me uncomfortable, because I am a grasshopper."

Louise knew as a child that she was a grasshopper when she realized that though she greatly admired her mother—a woman whose linen closet was a work of art and whose home was kept in immaculate order–she was not at all like her mother. She did not feel the same urgency to operate on schedule. Instead, she felt a strong desire to "waste time" by drawing, thinking, even daydreaming. It drove her mother crazy. What would become of Louise?

What became of Louise is that she is now an instructor at Brigham Young University, a writer of juvenile fiction, and a popular lecturer. She finds that thinking and daydreaming are very much a part of her daily agenda. Yes, she sees a need to clean and run a household, too, but she handles those tasks differently from the way her mother handled them: Louise accents different aspects of the home arts.

Some might complain that ants work *harder* than grasshoppers, but, Louise declared, "Grasshoppers work *differently* from ants." She rewrote the ending of the story of the grasshopper and the ants like this:

"It is winter, and the grasshopper is walking in the snow, talking to herself and answering herself. She wears a yellow slicker over her sweater because she can't find her parka (which is buried in the debris under her bed). Because she was out of groceries this morning, she is eating a brownie with a carton of milk bought at the 7-Eleven which, thank heaven, is open 365 days a year.... The door in the tree where the ants live swings open. The queen ant appears and says to the grasshopper, 'We're bored to death. Won't you tell us a story or at least a good joke? Our teenagers are driving us crazy; maybe you could write them a play to perform, or just a roadshow? Do you have any ideas for the daddy-daughter party?'

"The grasshopper replies that she has ideas for all of them. So the ant invites her in and seats her at a spotless kitchen table with pencil and paper, and the grasshopper writes the roadshow.

"The ant feeds her guest a slice of homemade bread, fresh from the oven, and a glass of freshly squeezed orange juice. 'How do you get all of these ideas?' she asks the grasshopper.

" 'They come to me,' says the grasshopper, 'while I am taking long hot baths.' " (In *A Heritage of Faith* [Salt Lake City: Deseret Book Co., 1988], p. 190.)

Because there are obviously even more than just two kinds of people in the world, Louise's message is very important. No, we aren't all the same, but that's okay—we don't need to be. There's room in this world for all kinds of people. Sometimes, it's true, we forget that it's okay to be different because there are so many things that we are advised to do. We may feel guilty and frustrated in our uniqueness because we think we're expected to fit a particular mold. So how do we handle all those injunctions we are given?

In the *Ensign* a few years ago, Dolores Ritchie gave a perceptive answer to the question we've all asked: "How is it possible to do *all* the things that are asked of us, especially when we have so little time to do it all in?"

Sister Ritchie suggested that we remember that the injunctions we receive are both *universal* and *particular,* "universal in that they are worthy of consideration by members of the Church universally; and particular in that they must be responded to by individuals of varying abilities, constraints, and needs.

"Our challenge is to decide which of all these possibilities we should focus on right now (keeping in mind that some — like prayer and exercise — are absolutely necessary for our spiritual and physical well-being).

"Meeting that challenge is neither simple nor immediate. Each of us must earnestly and honestly evaluate our priorities and our present opportunities for growth and service. Once we have decided what is most important in our lives and what is not so important, we will be able to make wise decisions about how to spend our time. We will also be able to decide how we can best use our unique gifts to bless our own lives and the lives of others.

"The scriptures teach us that 'to every man is given a gift,' but that not all have the same gifts. (See D&C 46:11.) Some members feel that they must be involved in *every* good effort and work for *every* gift; but such an attitude will usually result in paralyzing frustration. I like to think that there is a selective process in creating a life and a life's work that is analogous to creating a beautiful painting. Since trees are so majestic, I must have one in my painting; and who could leave out the mystery of fog, the texture of pearls, the sinewy torso of lion, the luminous emerald green of meadow after rain, the iridescence of goldfish, the vermillion of sky at twilight, the encircling arm of a mother? With so much beauty and goodness, I cannot fail to create a perfect work of art — and all within one frame! 'Overload' works no better in life than it does in art." (*Ensign*, July 1981, p. 33.)

As Sister Ritchie has so eloquently suggested, with the help of the Spirit we can each determine how to best develop our lives through the gifts we have been given. We have the right and the responsibility to decide what we wish to simplify and what we wish to elaborate in our lives as well. We can assess those areas in which we wish to focus at various times in our lives.

We can determine, because of our unique and individual personalities, styles, and strengths, how we can best function from day to day and week to week.

How we decide to manage our obligations and responsibilities is a personal matter between us and the Lord. I recognize that management is a constant challenge, but with his help we can determine what works best for us in our particular circumstances. What works for some might not work for others.

One woman I'm acquainted with, for instance, outlines her entire month into fifteen minute segments. She likes knowing exactly what she will be doing each minute of the day and doesn't mind scheduling everything carefully. In fact, she functions best that way. Such a detailed plan doesn't work for everybody. It would, in fact, drive some women crazy. Judy is one who comes to mind. Judy manages her affairs by doing her chores in marathon proportions. Rather than doing her wash daily or even weekly, she prefers doing it once a month. She hires some neighborhood girls and together they spend many hours sorting, folding, and matching. It is extremely fortunate that one of Judy's talents is budget shopping because one can only imagine how many stacks of pants, shirts, blouses, socks, and underwear it would take to keep four kids dressed between such widely spaced wash days.

Judy also likes to cook in bulk. When she cooks, it looks as if she is cooking not only for an army but for the navy and the air force and the marines as well. Then she freezes all this food. During the month, she pulls out her own homemade TV dinners any time she needs them. Judy's system may seem inconceivable to some, but what does that matter if it works for her?

Our minds all work differently, so we won't necessarily find management successes in the same ways. Some people function well with many things going on at the same time. Others, like Judy, like to focus heavily on one area before they move to something else.

When it comes to how we organize ourselves and our homes, we may also find that what works well for one person doesn't necessarily work as well for someone else. I knew that I could not organize my files by using the detailed numbering system an organization expert recommended because I knew that I would never keep it up. (And it gave me a headache!) Instead, I organized my files by using a much more simple alphabetical system, which I felt would be much easier to continue working with and which I felt would function fine in my home.

Because of our leanings and gifts, there may also be things in our lives we wish to hurry through in the homemaking arts so that we can slow down and take more time with other things. One woman, for instance, may enjoy thoroughly the art of hostessing and doesn't mind taking the time and making the effort, while another finds it so stressful and hard on her blood pressure that she either takes her guests out or orders in pizza!

One homemaker may wish to simplify gardening to the basics because she has little free time and would rather spend that in her sewing room, whereas another enlarges her garden and fills her yard with much produce and colorful flowers. Still another woman might find it works for her to emphasize gardening during one season and sewing at another, remembering that there are seasons of the year and seasons of life as well. Another homemaker might find it necessary to simplify quite a few areas of housekeeping to the mere basics because she has her hands full with small children or a job. And then there are women who simplify housecleaning or even get help because of other strong talent areas they feel inspired to pursue.

There are all kinds of "good" homemakers, and there are all kinds of "good" mothers. I like to read about famous people and was delighted with the biography of Madame Curie. She had planned to devote her life to science when she met and fell in love with a fellow scientist. Madame Curie was not what you could call a child bride when she married at the age of thirty-five. At thirty-six she became a first-time mother. Neither was she what you could call a conventional parent. Yet, in her own way, she was a superb mother who raised her daughters in an atmosphere of learning and dedication to science. She blessed their lives with her gifts.

In a Mother's Day program in my ward, several ward members were asked to tell briefly about their mothers and how they had blessed their lives. One sister spoke of a mother who had trained in nursing and willingly shared her skills and her gifts of compassion through loving service to neighbors. Another spoke of a mother who was highly creative and interested in drama and the arts. She gave her children much freedom to explore and use their imaginations. One brother spoke of a mother who blessed her children with her highly efficient and predictable management ability. I told about my own mother, who was highly unpredictable. For instance, I was never sure if we'd get to where we planned to go in the car because, to my embarrassment, my mother would stop and give people rides. No, she wouldn't offer rides to hitchhikers, just to older people who had too much to carry or people she thought might have just missed the bus. She also picked up stray dogs so she could find their owners. I told of my mother's ability to handle a hammer and saw with the same expertise she handled a sewing machine and that she enjoys searching for things to fix.

As we told about these completely different mothers, it was obvious that all of us regarded ours as successful and terrific.

There are many kinds of aunts, sisters, and grandmothers, and all kinds of employees as well. Although we can't always find jobs in precisely the areas we'd like, I'm sure many a business owner has been thankful for the employee who says "Let's see how I can best help this company succeed through my particular gifts," rather than, "How much can I get out of this business without giving anything back?"

When it comes to any kind of service, there are many ways to serve. Although I want to stress that sharing warm loaves of bread or anything out of the oven is a tremendous way to serve (one of my neighbors who does wonderful things with yeast sends them over once in a while, and I would not want to discourage her in any way!) we can contribute and lend assistance in a wide variety of ways.

When a sister I love lost her brother, I was dumbfounded. I spent several hours in my kitchen trying to bake but was disappointed (as I often am) at the results and did not feel the product qualified. Finally, I sat down and wrote this sister a poem that expressed my feelings. She seemed to appreciate that poem and made the comment afterwards that no one had ever written a poem just for her before.

A friend who likes to take pictures once handed me a photograph of our children dancing. I really appreciated this thoughtful gesture because I had forgotten my own camera that night.

Simply giving of our friendship is a gift we are all capable of giving. Kathy, who is especially good at it, has done great good and provided much therapy for a number of people just by talking to them on the phone. With her natural wisdom and understanding, her gift of knowing just the right words to say that will help, her willingness to let people talk through their frustrations; and her reliance on the Spirit, she has aided many a frenzied neighbor and fellow sister.

Even in church service we need not all be the same. In fact, I found out that it's probably best if we don't try to be. I learned that lesson when I taught a Young Women's class I took over from another teacher. She had been an expert at producing clever and adorable handouts. Because she had been such a good teacher, I assumed that her way was the way it was done and that I'd better do the same.

For the next few weeks I struggled for hours trying to think of wonderful craft items I could send home with the girls. I spent much time running around town trying to find such things as pom-poms and walnut shells. Then I spent much energy trying through trial and error to make those handouts look adorable. They rarely did, and preparing them was a miserable experience. Finally, after I'd been teaching only a short time, I realized that I was spending all my time on these handouts and not nearly enough time on the meat of the lessons — the main part. I also realized that I wasn't contributing my best by trying to be like this other sister, who loved crafts and who actually enjoyed preparing handouts. Finally, I said to myself, "I'm not my sister [in this case, sister in the gospel]. I'm me!"

I immediately began simplifying my handouts or skipping them altogether if they weren't essential. I used that added time to concentrate on thoroughly understanding the lesson material. When I took more time to prepare, I soon felt myself more in tune with the Spirit because he was better able to work through me. And with the Spirit, I soon felt able to teach through my own talents and in my own individual style.

As we think back in our lives, it isn't difficult to remember all kinds of visiting teachers, primary teachers, mutual teachers, choristers, Relief Society presidents, bishops, and others who led and inspired. Were they all the same? No, they enhanced their callings through their own unique strengths and personalities.

After teaching a Sunday School course on the presidents of the Church, I realized that there have also been all kinds of prophets at the head of our church. They've been unique in their styles, personalities, strengths, and gifts, even though they were all righteous instruments for the Lord.

The Twelve Apostles and other Church authorities today complement each other through their various backgrounds, skills, and gifts as well, and they are able to serve the Lord and act on his behalf through these gifts and strengths.

We don't need to wonder, then, if it is acceptable to the Lord when we are not exactly the same and when our gifts and leanings differ. He, in fact, has told us that it is through these differences that we contribute to the building of the kingdom. After he spoke of the different gifts we each have, he added, "for to some is given one and to some is given another that all might be profiteth thereby." (D&C 46:12.)

Chapter 5

See What God Hath Done

I used to wonder sometimes how we could inherit certain qualities from our ancestors but also have the strengths and gifts and personality traits that we had before we came to earth. Then I read an item by Dr. James O. Mason in the April 1974 *Ensign:* "Geneticists believe that the variations produced by chromosomal division and recombination may be a matter of chance. . . . But can the genetic code, with its unlimited variability, be intelligently programmed by understanding an application of divine law so that chance is not the determining factor? And is it possible that variation is being intelligently controlled to relate to our premortal development so that the physical body would develop not only to look like the spirit but to have the physical and character attributes that correspond to an eternal personality?" (P. 21.)

Dr. Mason's comment made me aware of one way that our Father in Heaven might use to continue to create us. I also realized that talents and strengths could be considered "gifts" from a loving Father because they are prepared and provided for us through his infinite wisdom and divine intelligence.

How much easier it is to appreciate our talents and

strengths when we think of them as blessings. Who, upon receiving a gift says, "Oh, this old thing?" We're much less likely to take our abilities and strengths for granted and much more likely to appreciate them when we think of them as gifts and blessings—which they *are.*

Consequently, we are also more ready to "see" them. I found this to be true with people I talked to. One woman, who was in a particularly sorry state, simply could see nothing—nothing whatsoever—that was good about herself. I suggested that she brainstorm with a sheet of paper in front of her and write down everything she could possibly think of that was good about herself—all strengths, even those of good health, such as good eyesight or strong muscles.

"I wear glasses and I have a bad back," she said.

I handed her a page from my binder. "Here. I know you can think of some things. Write down everything you think of during the next few days. Remember, we're talking about *everything.*"

"Why give me this paper when a ticket stub would do?" she asked.

She might as well have had a ticket stub for all the writing she had done when I saw her again. That's when I felt inspired to change my approach.

"Could it be that you're thinking of your strengths and talents and abilities as credits to you, when maybe you ought to be thinking of them as blessings you're thankful for—things you're grateful your Heavenly Father gave you? How can we expect Heavenly Father to bless us if we don't appreciate what he's already given us?"

Apparently she hadn't thought of her strengths and abilities in this way, and she looked surprised and a little embarrassed.

I suggested she put on her appreciation glasses this time and really look. It took time—blindness of this kind is a bad habit that needs to be broken — but gradually this woman began to see more assets in herself.

With our appreciation glasses on, it seems our eyes are opened much wider and we feel more comfortable about looking for our gifts.

As a matter of fact, as we look more closely at humility — that quality that we feel we must have and are admonished to have — we see that it really doesn't entail blindness. Christ knew exactly who he was and was well aware of his power. He was completely humble, and yet he spoke with power and authority. He was able to fulfill his purpose with great courage and dedication because he knew he had the power to do so. It seems entirely possible to recognize our strengths and powers and appreciate our magnificence as children of God and still be humble.

What, then, *is* humility? Let's look at Christ's life again. In one instance he said, "Be ye therefore perfect, even as your father which is in heaven is perfect." Throughout his life Christ gave credit not to himself but to his Father in Heaven. Glory to his Father, we sense, was his purpose. Could humility be the willingness to recognize the source of our powers, abilities, and strengths? Could it simply be giving credit where credit is due?

Doctrine and Covenants 59:12 tells us that our Father in Heaven is displeased with those who "confess not his hand in all things." If we are to express our gratitude and give credit where credit is due for our Father's gifts to us, then we have to identify what those gifts are. Acknowledging our gifts is a righteous endeavor, not an unrighteous one. And who can better help us identify our gifts than he who gave them to us?

Through prayer and the spirit of truth, we can see ourselves more fully and more clearly. Heavenly Father can help us see a brighter vision of who we are and thus how we can best serve him. Surely he wants us to have a healthy esteem and respect for ourselves, who we are, and what we've been given. Such respect leads us to have belief in ourselves and in our powers to progress. Confidence and humility do not conflict.

After we have solicited the help of our Heavenly Father and asked him for the assistance of the spirit of truth, we need to do our part as well. We have been told through scripture that a good way to discover an answer to a problem is to pray for help but that we must also search it out in our minds. The scripture passage "Seek and ye shall find" can apply to the discovery of our best selves as we seek through the Spirit and through conscious effort to acknowledge what Heavenly Father has given us.

What is the best way to make this conscious effort? Here are some steps you can take (they are based on an approach by Dr. Herbert Otto). These steps have worked for others and can help you "count" your blessings or inventory all that you have when it comes to powers, abilities, strengths, and leanings.

Step One

Begin listing on a sheet of paper or in a notebook talents and strengths as you think of them. A talent is any ability or power; a strength is any strong point. Remember that something you particularly enjoy doing or have a leaning toward may be counted as a strength. Think about your daily activities to determine what you do well or enjoy doing. Try to recall things you did well or enjoyed doing in past jobs, volunteer work, chores or responsibilities, service of any kind, classes, schooling, training, and so on. Analyze past successes or highlights in your life to determine the strengths related to them.

Here are some headings to help you start your search. Write down the headings and then list the strengths you see in yourself. Remember, however, that the headings and examples are only to give you ideas and can't possibly cover all your strengths and talents. Make up more headings as you discover more of your gifts. Keep in mind, as well, that some gifts won't fit into any particular category.

1. Physical talents or strengths

a. Strengths of appearance or good health, such as a pleasant smile, attractive voice, good eyesight, strong limbs, a keen sense of smell

b. Sports, or indoor or outdoor recreational activities you enjoy or in which you have some skill from table tennis to various forms of dance — even walking

c. Other kinds of special physical abilities or skills that take physical coordination or ability such as driving a car with a stick shift or typing

2. Cultural or artistic talents or strengths

a. Hobbies or crafts you enjoy, such as stamp collecting (or any other collecting), photography, ceramics, quilting: anything you spend time doing or have gained ability in

b. Expressive arts such as writing, drawing, design, playing a musical instrument, singing, dramatics, speech

c. Domestic or consumer arts such as cooking, decorating, sewing, gardening

d. Aesthetic strengths or talents such as the ability to feel appreciation for the out-of-doors, art, beauty of any kind

3. Intellectual strengths or talents

a. Academic interests or special aptitudes in subjects such as English, math, business, history, foreign language or culture, geography, philosophy, science, politics or government, psychology, sociology, computer science, engineering, mechanics

b. Strengths or interests related to such subjects that are more applied, such as the ability to budget well, interest in animals or a particular kind of animal, nutrition, medicine, the stars, Indian relics, poetry, folktales, dealing with teens

4. Talents of the mind (as identified by Dr. Calvin Taylor)

a. Wisdom or common sense: the ability to use good judgment

b. Originality: the ability to be innovative or creative

c. Forecasting: the ability to see possible problems ahead of time

d. Decision-making: the ability to make decisions and help others make decisions

e. Planning: the ability to organize well, remember details, or help others organize activities or programs

f. Communication: the ability to express thoughts to others or help them understand information

These talents of the mind may be talents in general for you or you may have them in specific fields or subjects and not in others.

5. Personality and character strengths or talents

a. Character traits. Refer to the adjectives listed on pages 17 through 19 and list all those you think apply to you

b. Qualities that you see in yourself when you're with someone who brings out the best in you or when you are in a comfortable or inspiring setting or atmosphere

c. Social talents or strengths such as the ability to be on good terms with family members, ability to put people at ease, etc.

6. Spiritual talents or strengths

a. Injunctions or commandments that come easily and naturally

b. Gifts you see in yourself that are talked of in scripture such as mercy, compassion, chastity; or specific spiritual gifts such as the gift of tongues, healing, great faith, etc.

c. Strengths or talents brought to your attention through daily experiences or life's experiences

d. Strengths in the form of leanings toward or involvement and help in causes or in any form of doing good

e. Gifts brought to your attention in patriarchal or other blessings

7. Other talents

Any strengths, interests, or leanings that don't fit into any one particular category or that fit into several categories, such as the ability and patience to fix things and ability to laugh at yourself.

Step Two

Now ask several people — at least three and preferably five (or more!) — who know you well to list the main strengths and talents they've seen in you. Often others see strengths in us that we miss. Add these strengths to your list.

Step Three

After you have made your list, keep it handy and continue adding to it over a period of several weeks or months.

Keep in mind that we get better at tuning in as we continue to work at it. Hints all around us can remind us of strengths and talents we have: the shops we choose to window shop in; where we enjoy spending free time, even what we think about when we don't need to be thinking; subjects that interest us in everyday conversation; what we are doing when time seems to fly; what part of the library we head for; and which sections of the newspaper we turn to.

When a friend was having trouble listing her strengths, I suggested we empty her handbag.

"It's a total mess," she said.

"That's okay," I said. "A messy handbag shows you're alive."

We discovered that most of the extra papers were pictures her children had drawn and games she had played with them.

She admitted that she is pretty good at thinking of fun things for her kids to do in spare minutes, and she was even able to admit she is a good mother who tries hard. We decided that her children's artistic talent may have come from her.

We also discovered that her coupons were neatly organized and filed meticulously, indicating care in budgeting. A small book of scripture reminded her that she finds great delight in studying the scriptures and has a deep love for them. There was a planning book with reminders. Her goals were listed carefully. That she is a planner, was obvious. A notation listed in one of the margins gave another clue to a great gift: "Help someone each day," it said. "Help lift someone's load."

You just never know what talents you'll find in yourself until you look for them!

Chapter 6

Polishing Up

Once we have inventoried our talents and have a good overview of who we are and what gifts we've been given, our eyesight improves dramatically. Our eyes can be opened even wider and our ability to recognize our gifts increases even more when we remember that when it comes to talents, there are different levels of development. In other words, even if we are not glowing in complete and perfect excellence in a particular area yet, we don't need to cross it off. A talent or gift in its beginning stages may not be wondrously beautiful yet, but it is still a talent or gift.

I remember as a beginning writer feeling discouraged at my own efforts after reading a fine piece in a magazine. What made me think I had talent to write? A few years later, after more training and work, I too was able to publish in that same magazine.

Sometimes it is simply added experience or exposure that is required. Several years ago, I asked Francis Urry, a dramatist who played President Lorenzo Snow in the film *Windows of Heaven* whether he had always had great natural talent in drama and speech. He told me that in the beginning he had used a flamboyant and highly inappropriate oratorical style. After auditioning with a teacher he hoped would accept him, he learned that his approach was old-fashioned and pompous. "Why do you try to sound as if you're preaching?" she asked him.

Brother Urry was helped to see that the goal of a reader is not to draw attention to himself but to interpret the written word so accurately that the listener is conscious only of the material being read, not of the reader. Just that bit of enlightenment changed Brother Urry's approach. He began studying such techniques of interpretation as pitch placement. He listened to tape recordings of his speaking to determine if he was stressing the right words. In time, he developed his skill and became an expert in his field.

Much is said about persistence, but perhaps just as important is patience with ourselves and with our progress and development. How can we acquire more of this patience with ourselves? Simply coming to terms with the fact that things do take time and expecting them to take time can help. Whenever we get disgusted with the slowness of our efforts and unhappy we're not moving ahead with full force in an area, it can help immensely to whisper to ourselves, "Things Take Time," and again recognize and acknowledge that few worthwhile things come at once.

A Dutch brass pitcher taught me another helpful aid when it comes to patience. The pitcher was tarnished with age, but I was pretty sure that there was a gleam underneath. I began to wonder, however, after I had rubbed polishing solution on the entire piece for a full ten minutes. There was nothing but grotesque smearing. The ugliness did not go away even with harder, more diligent rubbing and intense effort. Maybe I was kidding myself and this pitcher wasn't real brass.

Then I had an idea. Instead of rubbing the entire pitcher all at once, I began concentrating on a small two-inch portion. I rubbed that small section with my cloth until, sure enough, it was glowing richly. My elation at that small success made me want to continue to another two-inch portion, and then another. Each section of glow motivated me to go on to the next until at last the entire pitcher was glowing luminously. I placed it proudly on the table in the front entry, and I still take pleasure in looking at it.

If we set small, intermediate goals for ourselves to make sure we have successes along the way, we will find ourselves much more excited and inspired to continue in our development. An article published in the *New Era* several years ago called "How to Eat an Elephant" made the point that even the seemingly impossible can be accomplished one step at a time. Obviously, we don't just walk up to an elephant and bite it on the trunk. There are some intermediate steps involved. Eventually, however, it is possible to eat an elephant.

We can also learn patience as we learn to concentrate less on the goal of what we term success in a particular area (which can be evasive) and more on the process itself.

At a fireside I attended, the speaker drew an X on the top of a mountainside and said that though it's important to be looking up and have a direction when we hike, it is easy to get so caught up with attaining the goal that our stomachs churn and we don't stop to rest. Soon we suffer in pain and unmanageable fatigue. We may even give up because we realize that the cost is too high and the disappointment too great, especially when we discover that what we assumed was the top peak is just the first of many. "The wise hiker," said the speaker, "aims upward, yes, but enjoys the hike."

How can we enjoy the process of development more? On a hike we can notice the beauties along the way: the greenness of the pine trees, the freshness of the air, just the refreshing feeling of the out-of-doors and the invigoration of the walk itself. Likewise, we can enjoy the process of developing a talent or strength. I first found out that learning can be enjoyed when

I was a freshman at the University of Utah. During the first quarter, I was overcome with fear because of the pressures to succeed I had placed on myself. I began to panic, and my brain became paralyzed. After flunking my first midterm and getting a D on the second, I decided I'd better seek a counselor's advice. "Quit worrying about tests or grades," he said. "Just learn for the joy of learning. Think of the opportunity you have here! This is a mecca of information, an oasis of knowledge! This is your chance of a lifetime to immerse yourself in the educational process. Take advantage of it. Lap it up! Relish it! Love it!"

I'd never in my life thought of learning or training as something that could be enjoyed, but as he spoke I caught the vibrations of his enthusiasm. The more I thought about it, the more I realized that learning *was* something I could enjoy. As I began thinking differently about my training, I gradually found myself anxious to get up in the morning, anxious to study and acquire knowledge. Good grades became a by-product of this new joy. Even though I was no smarter, I found that I was doing better scholastically. The process of development, I had discovered, can be satisfying in itself.

Remember how eager and teachable we were as children? That child is still there, deep within us. We can again feel the joy in learning that we felt as children when we take pressures off ourselves. We can train ourselves to be filled with the wonder that replaces fear.

Getting in touch with our childlike joy in learning helps us eliminate pride from our lives. Pride, the universal sin President Ezra Taft Benson has warned us about, is a destroyer of progress and development. Whenever we refuse to learn something new for fear of getting caught looking awkward or less than excellent, we shackle ourselves. The notion that after a certain age we must already know everything and do everything seriously curtails our development. How fearful we adults are of starting at the bottom! Yet the bottom rung on a ladder is the best place to get a beginning foothold. It's extremely tricky to start at the second rung from the top of a ladder. It's difficult, too, to leap to the middle of the mountainside to begin a hike. Recognizing that we have a way to go before we will be proficient is something difficult to accept. We'd rather already be halfway there.

Ben, the main character of *Corker,* the novella I wrote several years ago, wanted to take up running. He didn't want to start out by running a block or two; he wanted to run three miles immediately. After all, his "puny" neighbor Darlene ran that far every day. Ben soon discovered that for him, however, running three miles was out of the question. He felt like a running waterbed and collapsed after three blocks.

Proud of his masculinity and his macho image, Ben felt that being able to run only three blocks was unacceptable. He decided to quit before he made an even bigger fool of himself. Then his sister reminded him that three blocks was absolutely remarkable for someone in his condition. Once he swallowed his pride, he was able to progress. Pride really doesn't taste so bad going down.

Teachability is another important element of humility. How beautiful is the person who thirsts for learning and progressing and doesn't care what others think or who knows it. Youth is eternal as we overcome the pride that makes us old.

When Francis Urry was told he was using an outdated oratorical style, he could have responded, "How dare you?" He could have walked out in a huff. Instead, he was open to learning and eager to correct his style.

Learning the art of nurturing ourselves can also aid us in feeling good in the process and wanting to develop and continue. We're told to love ourselves, yet often we are harder on ourselves than we are on anyone else. We rip our efforts and toss them into the trash. We verbally attack ourselves over mistakes. We become angry at ourselves and even call ourselves names. We say things to ourselves that we wouldn't dream of saying to someone else who is going through the development process. Yet, who can get ahead without making mistakes once in a while? We all have moments when we seem to be taking giant steps backward and moments when we feel awkward and ugly during our development.

More joy and patience can come as we learn to be gentle to ourselves and learn to encourage ourselves. We can give ourselves small rewards. We can give ourselves a pat on the back once in a while and say to ourselves, "You're doing just fine. Okay, so you made a mistake; now you'll know next time."

There is, after all, no end to development and progress, so we might as well learn to enjoy it.

More joy can come as we allow ourselves to rely on our Father in Heaven and feel his love as well. As we endeavor to stay close to the spirit of comfort and truth and inspiration, we will find ourselves able to progress in the best ways. Fortunately, even when we don't love ourselves, Heavenly Father still does. He can help us feel a godlike peace and patience. And because he has asked us to develop our gifts, surely he will be there to help us.

Perhaps we should keep in mind, as well, that because we are all unique, development comes differently for each of us. We don't all need to reach a predetermined level to be successful. Not all who want to develop their talent for writing need to become Shakespeares or even publish to find success. Not all artists need become Van Goghs. With any talent, our development is as individual as we are.

What we can *all* discover by looking back is that our development didn't take nearly as long as we thought it was taking. Just a step or two a day, we find, can add up to more than 365 steps a year. And didn't we learn from that plucky little tortoise in one of Aesop's fables that slow and steady gets us ahead?

No matter how slow progress seems at the time, when we look back we find it was there, just the same. We often find, in fact, that it was significant. The adolescent who had so much trouble communicating and wanted so badly to talk easily with people and know what to say now has to be careful not to talk too much. The homemaker who dropped stitches in the beginning of her needlecraft efforts is now knitting gorgeous sweaters; the pianist who thought she'd never learn the chords is accompanying a youth choir; and the sister who didn't dare get up in front of people is her ward's Relief Society president. "Genius," said an inspired Elbert Hubbard, "is only the power of making continuous effort."

Chapter 7

The Greatest Tragedy

"What you are is God's gift to you; what you do with yourself is your gift to God." When I first heard that statement, I assumed it meant developing and magnifying the talents we've been given and not consciously burying them, as did the servant in the parable of the talents. But then I realized that no amount of development is a gift to God if that gift isn't used for good. In fact, the way we use our gifts is probably more important than how wonderfully developed they are. It is reassuring to recognize that small abilities or powers or strengths used for good are of greater value to our Father in Heaven than highly polished talents or great gifts that are not used for good.

Sadly, we see the misuse of talents all around us. What a tragedy that is. Gifts that could be used to inspire, uplift, and better our world, are instead used to further Satan's purposes. Such misuse, we quickly recognize, is even more tragic than the failure to use our gifts.

Why do people sometimes misuse their talents? Often they misuse them out of a desire for money, fame, power, and so on. Greed, for instance, can cause people to want to give less than their best. Quality is downplayed for profit, and dishonesty creeps in as well. People feel tempted to say whatever it will take to acquire that dollar!

And what could be a more flagrant example of the misuse of talents for dollars than that insidious vice we call pornography? The talents of writing, photography, or cinematography are misused to victimize others, dulling senses, belittling and demeaning and addicting others to its venomous poison through magazines, books, films, and television. We see the unacceptable appear to become acceptable to our society.

It is easy for us to recognize when others so flagrantly abuse their talents, and it is our responsibility to speak out when we see that happening.

It is also our responsibility to guard against our own misuse of talents, which may be less easy to recognize. One abuse of talents I can think of right away is giving less than our best because of greed. An experience I had showed me just how easily the green-backed monster of greed can seduce us into giving less than our best.

Several years ago, the family income wasn't stretching quite far enough to meet the flood of bills the family had recently incurred. Writing workshops, I thought, just might be the answer. To find out what I was up against, I took out a piece of paper and a pencil and did some quick figuring. I discovered that even if I had only five students and charged a minimal amount, I'd be able to bring in about twenty-five or thirty dollars per session.

It sounded good. It sounded so good that I decided that I would manage carefully enough to teach two such sessions per week, thus getting more mileage out of my preparation time. At twenty-five dollars or so per session, I'd make about fifty dollars a week, or two hundred dollars a month.

Not bad, but it still didn't quite cover what we needed, so I jotted down what would happen with eight students in each class. With eight students I could earn eighty to a hundred dollars a week, or nearly four hundred dollars per month.

"Goodness," I thought, "why not teach a class every day?"

Eagerly, I jotted down how much I would make per month teaching five workshops per week. "Eight hundred dollars or more! Not bad for a part-time job! What if I taught even more?"

My pencil flying, I figured out how much I would make teaching two classes a day. Well, why not? And perhaps I'd charge by the month so that anyone missing a class would not expect reimbursement. In fact, I could easily charge more than I'd originally thought.

Dollar signs dancing in my head, I continued. Three classes a day with twelve people; four classes a day with fifteen people; five classes a day with twenty people. I'd charge even more! I'd charge ten to fifteen dollars a session. People always appreciate what they have to pay for. If I charged more, they'd just figure they were really getting something. Maybe I'd charge twenty-five to thirty dollars a session. How about fifty? A hundred!

It was late evening by then, and I was getting bleary-eyed with all the figuring. In fact, I realized that I was calculating in the semidarkness. After turning on the overhead lamp, I refigured my computations, and then finally, reluctantly, I went to bed.

I didn't sleep long. I got up several times during the night to do more figuring. I found myself writing the same numbers over and over and over again. By this time my eyes had narrowed, and my breath was coming in spurts.

In the morning, the monster's tendrils were definitely gripping me. I skipped breakfast and didn't bother to get dressed because I had more high-finance figuring to do. "More," the green-backed monster was hissing in my ear. How many people could I possibly squeeze into my living room? How much could I possibly squeeze out of each? What if I held two or three workshops simultaneously? "More! More!" the monster chanted. Maybe I could seat people on the floor as well as on chairs. So what if they weren't comfortable.

"More! More! More!" It wasn't far into the morning when I began spending my money. I'd buy a fancy car. We'd been needing to redecorate for quite a while. And clothes. I really needed clothes. I pictured myself walking into a store and buying anything I wanted. And who wouldn't like to be able to do that? More purchasing power is everyone's dream. But difficult as it is to explain, it wasn't just purchasing power I was after any more. I wanted money just to have it; I wanted to collect it; I wanted to wallpaper with it.

"More! More! More!" I'd rent an assembly hall. A thousand people at two hundred and fifty dollars a session would bring in five hundred thousand dollars for two sessions. I could hardly breathe and my teeth were clenched together. Yet still the monster was whispering in my ear. It was important that I become a millionaire before I was thirty—no, a multimillionaire! I was worrying about tax shelters and thinking of buying a neighboring town when the telephone rang.

"Oh, hello!" How happy I was to hear from Audrey. She had at one time indicated a desire to learn more about writing. "It's funny you should call right now," I said, as I subconsciously plotted how I could convince my friend to turn over a huge portion of her income for my intense new craving. "I was just making plans to teach a writing workshop. Are you still interested?"

"That's great! I'd love to participate," Audrey said.

" 'That's great, I'd love to?' " I rubbed my hands together like Fagan in *Oliver Twist*. Why, this was easy!

But then Audrey bounced me back onto reality's stage with a rather pointed question. "What do you think you'll be teaching?"

"Excuse me?" I asked.

"What do you think you'll be teaching? I mean, what kind of writing? Fiction? Poetry?"

"Oh, yes, sure, ummm." Why was I sounding so awkward? I was sounding awkward, I realized, because that's exactly how I was feeling. The fact is I didn't have the slightest idea what I planned to teach. Oh, I had used many *many* legal-size sheets of paper and much mental strain discovering what I planned to *make*, but I had not devoted one brain cell of thought, not one square inch of paper, to what I'd be offering.

"Ummm, I'll tell you what. I'll get back with you when I've finished my planning," I said to Audrey. "I'll, umm, call you tomorrow."

"Sounds great," Audrey answered.

After I hung up the phone I stared at the stack of papers before me, each sheet bursting its borders with dollar signs. I shook my head and blinked. I rubbed my eyes. What on earth could have gotten into me? How could I have gotten so carried away that I had forgotten that first and foremost I needed to give fair service and have something to offer? I had spent hours figuring out how much money I'd be getting for my teaching when I didn't even have anything to give my students.

Quickly, I crumpled up the papers before me. At the same time I pulled loose from the monster's tendrils with a jerk. Tearing a new sheet of paper from the legal pad, I started writing again. This time words, not numbers, appeared on my sheet. The words suggested ideas and exercises that I hoped would benefit those who wanted to learn the art of writing. Gradually, I found myself scribbling with urgency again, but the urgency was different this time. A good feeling enveloped me. In fact, I was excited. I filled another sheet of paper with my scribbles, and then another. Soon I couldn't wait to teach — to share.

What a contrast this new, uplifting feeling was to the dark urgency I had felt earlier. Now I felt free. And in a sense, I was

free — free from the clutches of that green-backed monster —
greed.

That experience helped me realize how easy it is to be
consumed by greed and lust for money and how on guard we
must be to avoid the tendrils of the green-backed monster. In
today's world, where money has become the measuring stick
for success, its pursuit all-important, it is even easier to slip
into the monster's clutches.

In a commencement address at Brigham Young University
a few years ago, Dr. Hugh Nibley spoke of the perversion in
today's world: "The manager knows the price of everything
and the value of nothing because for him the value is the price.
Quality is downgraded in our world into what is saleable. But
this seems to be nothing new. Even in Christ's world it was
assumed that everything had a price." (See *BYU Today*, Feb.
1984.)

"But wait a minute," we might object, "perhaps money isn't
or shouldn't be everything in our lives, but it's still something.
We still need it to function. There's no such thing as a free
lunch, and dinner and breakfast are getting expensive as well.
Besides, what's wrong with wanting to get ahead in the world
as long as we keep our heads?"

It's true that we need to function financially. It isn't money,
itself, however, that is the culprit. It is only when we begin
thinking of it before other things that it becomes dangerous.

The irony here is that when we use our gifts for good and
have a caring attitude, other blessings do not necessarily evade
us. In talking with a friend about her children's braces, I asked
about her orthodontist and how she had made her choice. She
told me of one office in which she had felt as if she and her
daughter were herded through quickly, strictly for the purpose
of making money. The atmosphere seemed cold, and she was
immediately pressured to sign up all her children for the program. Whether they really needed braces or not didn't seem

to be a concern. At the office of the orthodontist she now goes to, however, her daughter was given careful attention by the doctor and his assistants. Although the charge was slightly more, she sensed that the doctor's interest was not so much in how much money could be made but first and foremost that her child's teeth would be properly analyzed, cared for, and worked with so that the result would be satisfactory. After I listened to her comments, I too was anxious to work with the people in the second office.

I once read about a clothing designer who stayed away from fads and the whims of fashion to create elegant clothes of lasting quality for his customers. He felt that by helping customers save money on such "classics" he was doing his part to help them. Did he have trouble finding customers? Of course not.

I found that when I began really caring about the people in my classes and about what I was teaching, when I did my best to give honest, genuine help, I had no trouble building my classes. Later, I wondered how much word of mouth business I would have gotten if I had herded people into my home with little thought for either their progress or their physical well-being.

We've already mentioned how much we appreciate those who are obviously working for more than just a paycheck. When my friend Carol came to my home to help me put up wallpaper, she stood there in my doorway, her equipment in hand, saying, "I'm here to help!"

We can all stand before our Father in Heaven with our "equipment," or gifts, and say, "I'm here to help! These are the gifts I've been blessed with. How can I best use them for thee?"

When Marjorie Holmes, the author of *Two from Galilee* was a high school student, her teacher, recognizing her gift, wrote a note on one of her essays. "There is a duty," it said.

Mrs. Holmes realized that the teacher was referring not only to her duty to develop her gift but to her duty to use it for good, and throughout her life she has done just that.

What we can find when we consecrate our gifts to the betterment of this world and the building of the kingdom is that the gifts we thought were so small seem to have magnified. There is a replenishing and strengthening process in giving our best and sharing and helping. We are reminded through scripture that "losing" ourselves is one of the best ways of "finding" ourselves. President Spencer W. Kimball added that it's easier to find ourselves because there's much more to find.

When we use our gifts for good, they glow and grow — and no wonder, when heavenly light is reflected from them. The teacher feels inspiration when she teaches with deep concern that her students grasp the message. The musician, no matter what her level of development, plays with feeling and power when she hopes to use her gift to share the inspiration of music's beauty. The artist creates more beautiful works than she thought possible when she seeks to uplift. All our gifts, whatever they may be, and whatever our level of development, are enhanced when we use them for good.

"Men and women who turn their lives over to God will discover that He can make a lot more out of their lives than they can," President Ezra Taft Benson said at one time. "He will deepen their joys, expand their vision, quicken their minds, strengthen their muscles, lift their spirits, multiply their blessings, increase their opportunities, comfort their souls, raise up friends, and pour out peace. Whoever will lose his life in the service of God will find eternal life." ("Jesus Christ — Gifts and Expectations," *Ensign*, Dec. 1988, p. 4.)

It seems clear, then, that when we endeavor to use our gifts for good, we will find so much more to give and blessings we can't even imagine.

Chapter 8

Weaknesses Can Become Strengths

How easy it is to see our weaknesses! Studies show that when given equal amounts of time to list both, the average person lists ten to fifteen times more weaknesses than strengths. Could that be because we feel more comfortable noticing our deficiencies? It is more socially acceptable to notice them, but could it also be that we are simply too hard on ourselves?

Dr. Otto implies that we may be labeling ourselves negatively too quickly when he suggests that in inventorying our strengths, we check our list of weaknesses as a possible source for strengths. Apparently we are so hard on ourselves that sometimes we label ourselves as weak in areas that are, in fact, just the opposite. Let me explain.

My friend Linda thinks it's extremely important to be a tough lady. She likes to feel strong and in control. None of this gushy, mushy stuff for her! That's why it bothers her a great deal when she finds herself getting teary at weddings or during other touching moments. "What's wrong with me?" she asks. "I'm blubbering like a fool again. I can't stand myself when I do this." The tendency for her eyes to water up seems a serious impairment to Linda. But is this "weakness" really a weakness? On the contrary, Linda's tears show the emotional strength she has of feeling deeply for others.

Another woman gets after herself for being a busybody and "interfering" in others' lives. Although it's true that getting involved is a negative trait if we're critical or gossipy about our findings, Mary uses her ability to notice what's happening for the express purpose of helping or lending support. What she terms nosy-ness is in reality an ability to sense needs.

"I talk on the phone far too much," Mary Ann says. It's true that Mary Ann does talk on the phone a great deal. Once she talked on the phone nearly all day. She also, in the process, literally saved the life of a friend who was deeply discouraged and had no one else to confide in.

In other words, a second, less critical look at some of our supposed weaknesses can be eye-opening. And even if our weaknesses aren't what we could consider strengths, they may still give us clues to strengths and abilities. A friend of mine pointed out to me one day that weaknesses or faults can actually be the flip side of strengths. "I try to remember whenever I get upset with my daughter for her ho-hum attitude when it comes to getting places on time and her general lack of concern about details, that this easy-going attitude also makes her easy to get along with, calm, not uptight or critical in relationships, and an all-around nice person to have around. On the flip side, she's pretty pleasant to have in our family *because* she doesn't get uptight as easily as some of the rest of us do."

Likewise, a friend who wonders what's wrong with her because her home isn't always as clean and neat as she'd like it to be *can* give herself credit for her flexibility, her patience when it comes to the creative messes her children make, and her emphasis on doing good and always being available immediately when someone needs help. Recognizing the flip sides of our weaknesses and seeing the whole picture can help us feel better about ourselves. And when we feel better, we're better able to progress and make the changes we need to make.

We may, of course, have weaknesses that don't seem to have a flip side. What can we do about them? Many times what we could think of as weaknesses can simply be ignored because they don't need to be in the picture. Even Christ, the master teacher, did not seem to feel it necessary to become proficient in everything. He became a carpenter by trade, but so far as we know he did not become an expert weaver as well. Even he had only so much time on this earth, and he zeroed in on what was most important for him to do in this life.

It is true, however, that sometimes we are asked to do things in precisely those areas where we struggle. We've probably all had callings in which we felt there had been a mix-up. When our ward was newly formed, the bishop called me to be the Relief Society cooking specialist. "With your baby due so soon," he said, "we wanted you to have a job that wouldn't be too much of a challenge."

Cooking specialist—easy? I knew it really wasn't appropriate to laugh when a bishop extends a calling, but a nervous coughlike chortle came out anyway. At that very moment there was an article in my typewriter called "Confessions of a Non-Gourmet" in which I carefully explained that we don't need to be marvelous at everything in order to be acceptable and that there's room for all kinds of people in our world, our community, and our church. Now the bishop was asking me to elaborate the very area I'd been simplifying in my life.

"Ummm, Bishop, you might not be aware that..." I explained that in my kitchen, if it tasted all right, it generally looked ghastly; and if it looked all right, it invariably tasted ridiculous. Rarely did the twain meet. "I'm hardly the woman for this job," I said. Then I told him about my article on the subject, which was ready to be typed in final form. The bishop agreed that I was in a rather humorous predicament and chuckled good-naturedly.

"But I'm sure you're exaggerating," he said. "I'm sure you're a fine cook."

"No," I assured him. I was not exaggerating, and by no stretch of the imagination could I be called a "fine" cook. I backed up my statement by describing my "jawbreaker" bread. I told him of the birthday cake whose frosting had puckered, which led to extremely messy and unfestive results.

"Besides," I said, "you'll have to agree it would look a little strange if the by-line on this article about how well I don't cook reads, 'Anya Bateman is cooking specialist in her Salt Lake ward.' " The bishop was really chuckling now and seemed to be enjoying the situation immensely. I was glad we were having such a good time. We both continued smiling, and I waited for him to rescind the call. He didn't.

"Well, Sister Bateman, it's up to you, of course, but we felt good about having you handle this assignment. Would you like to think about it?"

No, I thought. The truth was I really didn't want to think about it at all. But I sighed inwardly. Our ward was just new. With every position to fill, the bishop and his counselors had their hands full. Compassion alone should motivate me to accept the position. On top of that there was the guilt that was seeping in because of what I'd been taught about accepting callings *cheerfully*.

"Can you think of any ways you *could* handle this calling, Sister Bateman?"

"I suppose I could if I did some delegating," I said, mustering little in the way of cheer. "A lot of delegating."

I'll probably need to have the position catered, I thought to myself.

"However you'd like to handle the calling would be fine," he assured me. Then he added with a twinkle in his eye.

"Remember there's a scripture that tells us our weaknesses can be made strong."

"Could we settle for barely adequate?" I asked.

"Adequate would be fine," he answered quickly.

We've talked about emphasizing our talents and gifts in our lives. But what if we feel that we lack completely what is required? How do we handle callings or responsibilities in which we don't feel there is much, if anything, we can contribute?

When Craig was called to be the ward music director, his reaction was similar to mine. "Me, music director?" he gasped. "You've got to be kidding!" Not only had singing never been something Craig had emphasized in his life but it was something he tried to avoid. Craig did have other interests, though. He enjoyed Church history and had a keen interest in biographical anecdotes. Craig drew on this interest to talk about the composers of the hymns and what had prompted them to write the pieces. He also used his knowledge of the scriptures to give insights on how the hymns could be better applied to our lives. His unconventional approach inspired ward members to sing with great feeling. It wasn't until after his release that a ward member who happened to be sitting by Craig observed for the first time that he hadn't been kidding when he said he couldn't sing. He really couldn't sing. No one had noticed because they had been so enthralled with his presentations.

Even when we feel there is very little we can contribute to a calling, often we will surprise ourselves with what we can come up with. We can almost always magnify a calling *through* our unique gifts.

Unless we have inventoried our talents so that we are somewhat aware of what we do have to offer, we may find it difficult to understand the ways in which we can contribute.

That is why, as cooking specialist, I quickly looked to others

for help. I did just exactly what I told the bishop I would need
to do: I delegated. The first month, I had Sister Bybee show
us how to bake bread. I certainly didn't want to teach anyone
how to make my jawbreaker variety. The next month I asked
Sister Briggs to show us a cake decorator's secrets of frosting
and decorating cakes. It wasn't until the third month that it
occurred to me that I could share with the sisters some of the
easy, fast, and almost foolproof recipes I had collected over
the years. Perhaps others in the ward did not have that white
thumb of confidence in their kitchens either. We could *ex-
change* recipes. Even experts in the kitchen undoubtedly had
days when they needed quick, easy meals. I might be able to
teach one or two of the classes, after all.

I also recognized, as I prepared to teach my first cooking
class, that I had the ability to laugh at myself. Maybe I could
give comfort to others who had had catastrophes in their kitchens by letting them know they weren't alone.

It turned out that many sisters were interested. Not only
did we collect some excitingly easy recipes, but sure enough,
we had a great time comforting one another as we told of
kitchen misfortunes. It turned out that even some of the experts
had had catastrophes, and that gave the rest of us hope. Several
sisters, to my surprise, commented afterwards that this class
had really helped them. One said that having a novice teach
the course rather than an expert helped her feel less alone in
her plight.

And as is usually the case with a calling, it helped me more
than it helped anyone else. I had been leaning heavily on just
a few recipes, and now my repertoire of almost foolproof
recipes had almost tripled. I even learned some principles that
would help me handle the basics more adequately. For instance, I discovered that some of my fiascos had fascinatingly
simple explanations. Sister Bybee explained patiently that
"warming" the yeast does not mean boiling it and that bread

has a much less rocklike texture if the yeast is alive and flourishing. Sister Briggs suggested cooling my cakes (even freezing them) before frosting them for better results. By the time I was released from my calling just a short time later, I was feeling that maybe, just maybe, the bishop had been inspired after all.

Even if we serve through our strengths, however, we will undoubtedly find aspects to work on in order to do a competent job in a weak area. Craig, realizing it helps a great deal if a chorister knows how to lead music, no doubt got a quick refresher course on how to move his arm to three-quarter time. He solicited the help of others. He probably studied music lesson books and did some research. I too scouted out my old foods notebooks from school and studied children's cookbooks to get ideas.

We sometimes find a need to brush up our skills in some area in order to be proficient at it. I was delighted when I read a story of Madame Curie's life describing how this eminent scientist learned how to stir up goodies other than chemicals and, like all new mothers, learned the basics of warming bottles, changing diapers, and bathing babies. I got the impression she didn't mind a bit.

Whether it is a calling or a responsibility or another kind of service for which we find that our gifts don't meet the needs, we can discover when we seek Heavenly Father's help that miracles are possible.

If we turn ourselves over to him and say, "What do I do? I want to help, but I have no tools, no equipment, no know-how," we just may find ourselves being given the direction we need. And then, when we open our heart to his help and rely on him, what we need comes to us. The scriptures and everyday life are filled with examples of those who, in doing service, are amazed that through the Lord's help, they find themselves doing what they were sure they could not do. They find that where they thought they had only weaknesses, they had strengths, after all.

Sometimes it is simply the desire to develop in a weak area that prompts us to seek help and work for competence. What book about talents would be complete without mentioning the determined and persistent Heber J. Grant?

At first I doubted some of the stories I heard about President Grant. Oh, I could believe the story that said he learned to play baseball and ended up on a championship team. And I believed it when I heard that he attained beautiful penmanship, even though his handwriting had been called hen-scratching. But sing? I just couldn't bring myself to believe that someone who was tone deaf could ever learn to carry a tune. Singing, I believed, was an ability you either have or you don't.

With all due respect to President Grant, I believed that *he* sincerely felt he had learned to sing on key, but I had never heard a second opinion of his singing. Sometimes people think they're carrying a tune, and they are, but they're carrying it near Denver when they should be in Pittsburgh. Then I learned from an article by Joan Oviatt in the September 1984 *Ensign* that President Grant's ability to sing had been confirmed. Apparently, the very singing teacher who had told him bluntly and plainly that he would never be able to sing on key was forced to admit that President Grant sang "God Moves in a Mysterious Way" without a single mistake. The teacher said he couldn't comprehend it, but President Grant understood it perfectly. It didn't cost him just a little effort to learn to sing that hymn: he had sung it five thousand times! President Grant gave learning to sing his devoted and unfloundering effort. But perseverance was one gift he had plenty of.

Each time President Grant wanted to learn to sing a particular song, he practiced it more than a hundred times a day. An acquaintance of mine, a grandson of Joseph F. Smith, remembers traveling as a young boy with his grandfather and

President Grant. Because President Grant sang unceasingly, this friend acknowledges that his singing was not always pleasant. But President Grant persisted until he learned to hear when he was off key. Then he persisted until he learned how to get back on key.

President Grant withstood considerable ridicule in the process. One of his friends, Richard Young, suggested that although President Grant's point was a good one — "If *you* can learn to sing, nothing need discourage *anybody*" — he was perhaps improving his weakness at the expense of his reputation.

But did he give up? No, he took the jokes in stride and carried on with greater determination. Eventually President Grant learned to sing more than two hundred songs on key. For a man who couldn't carry a tune, learning to sing more than two hundred songs on key could be considered something of a miracle. But miracles, it seems, can happen through perseverance and determination.

Although it makes sense to focus on interests where there is some natural leaning or gift, I was amazed to discover the great number of people who claim that some of their best strengths — talents that are now focal points in their lives — were at one time weaknesses. Jean, for instance, a seamstress who performs wonders on a sewing machine, claims she had absolutely no interest in sewing at first. In fact, she disliked sewing. "Then how did you get so good at it?" I asked.

She explained that her sister had a business and needed help. Jean realized that sewing for her sister was work that she could do at home, so she pursued it. At first it was horrifying because she picked out more stiches than she sewed. But gradually she learned the tricks of the trade. Through perseverance, she gained expertise. "Now I love to sew. It's one of my best talents."

Elaine heads Salt Lake's Voluntary Action Center and coordinates hundreds of projects to aid those who are struggling.

When I visited with her I expected she would tell me that she had always loved rendering community service and that volunteering had been a natural leaning. To my surprise, she told me, "Church service seemed natural, but this other kind of service seemed foreign. Only when I was placed in a position to see an intense need did I feel an urgency to get involved. Now I love what I do."

One of my favorite people to talk with confessed that her ability to converse well hadn't come naturally either. She had always been extremely shy but recognized the need to learn the art of conversation when she trained in cosmetology. She loved doing hair, but she could see that she also needed to talk to the people whose hair she did. Consequently, she observed what others, who were good at conversing, said. She learned comments to make and questions to ask to spur interest. Even better, she became interested and empathetic, and eventually she became a wonderful person to talk with. She no longer practices cosmetology, but her "special" ability to converse well still brings much joy to friends and neighbors and family members.

What about the classic talents of art or music? I asked my neighbor Robert Rumel, a well-established Utah artist who teaches drawing and painting, how much natural talent he looks for in his students. "None," he said. He claims that he himself hadn't had any natural talent. In fact, as a child he had overheard his mother confide to a friend that she had hoped for an artistic child but had gotten Bob instead. If even a mother, one of those souls who can generally spot in her offspring the minutest and faintest flickering of talent, hadn't seen any, Bob must really not have had much. "Anyone can learn to draw," Bob claims. "Anyone."

Another neighbor seconded that opinion when she told me of an art class she took. The class was designed to prove that anybody can learn to draw by learning to *see*. She explained that the art teacher had had the students explain to her exactly how to draw an object they were looking at, line by line. Then the teacher followed their instructions to the minutest detail. It was her students' responsibility to make sure she drew each line correctly. In that way, they learned to see each portion of the object exactly as it was. After they had thoroughly observed the object, line by line, detail by detail, they drew it themselves, using the same process. "We tried it and it worked," said my neighbor. "By learning to really *see*, people who had never drawn in their lives were amazed to find themselves producing wonderful pictures."

Suzuki believed that skills in playing the piano and the violin can be learned through the art of listening. Thousands of children have proved him right.

"The French composer Claude Debussy showed little promise as a child; he lacked even the beginner's enthusiasm at the start of his training. Neither of his parents was musical, and it was not until a former pupil of Chopin heard the boy's half-hearted playing that any real effort was made to encourage him. For a long time, Claude found difficulty in mastering certain techniques of music, and his teachers were not impressed by his endeavors. But when he became interested, he developed into a serious and dedicated student, and his perseverance won out. Today he is recognized as the foremost pioneer of musical impressionism." (Sally Peterson Brinton, "Blessing Your Home with Music," *Ensign*, Mar. 1983, p. 38.)

Even creativity can be developed once we learn the basic principles. Peter Lassig, the gardener at Temple Square, told me about the beautiful and original gardening designs people in his workshops were able to create once they understood certain gardening and landscaping laws and principles. "There are a lot of Grandma Moseses out there," he said. "You can bring in someone off the street who has never even had a yard of his own, show him some basic principles of gardening design, and you'll be amazed what he can do."

Weaknesses, it seems, are often weaknesses only because we lack experience, know-how, or exposure. Sometimes they are areas in which we simply have never taken the time.

In *The Road Less Traveled*, Dr. Scott Peck told of passing a neighbor who was tinkering with a motor. Dr. Peck complimented his neighbor on his skill and made a comment about his own inadequacy with mechanics. "Oh, you're just not willing to take the time," his neighbor responded. Dr. Peck could not believe that something so simple could be true, yet when he tested the theory and really took the time to discover the solution to a mechanical problem in a client's car, he discovered that it was true. With enough time and study, he found he was not as helpless with engines as he had thought.

If it takes time to develop areas where there is some talent and know-how, obviously even more time will be required in areas where there is very little natural inclination. No, we don't need to take the time in every area, but it is still comforting to know that with sufficient time, we have possibilities even in some of those areas we have crossed off our list of capabilities to work on.

Good feelings come when we allow ourselves to begin at the beginning. Believe me, I was never excited about cooking just after I had cooked something ridiculous. But my failures could have been caused by my always trying to skip over essentials. I thought I needed to be "creative," and I felt too proud to follow directions carefully. Considering how little knowledge of basic principles I had, it is no wonder things rarely turned out. I hadn't been willing to begin at a lower level. When I did look for recipes, I looked for them in complicated cookbooks for advanced cooks. These recipes included such statements as "knead the bread to the right consistency" (What was the right consistency?"), or "stir until properly thickened" (How thick is that?). The undertone of these directions read, "We wouldn't want to insult your intelligence." I was too proud to admit that I needed my intelligence insulted. I needed to be told such things as "Don't boil the yeast!" Once I swallowed my pride and found my level in children's cookbooks — which gave directions and hints that I could understand — I began to make progress.

Beginning at the beginning may even mean starting at a remedial level. And that's not so bad. As I learned basic principles, and as I swallowed my pride and began following directions carefully, I began having successes once in a while. The other day I actually made a fairly decent birthday cake. No, it didn't have fancy roses, but it wasn't puckered, either! Miraculously, it tasted fine too. That experience has given me hope.

Joy can be developed in an area as we become familiar with it. Just as we can learn to love people more when we find out about them and get to know them better, we can learn to feel leanings toward pursuits we thought we'd never like.

We do, of course, need to remain realistic. Physical limitations should be taken into consideration. In general, excellence is not as accessible in some things if we weren't born with natural gifts. Heber J. Grant didn't try to join an opera company or sing opera. He just endeavored to sing some of the hymns on key.

Even where natural gifts seem lacking, however, it is amazing what desire can do. The daughter of an acquaintance, a college student who was heading back to school after vacation, expressed to me her excitement at having been one of three freshmen picked to sing in the college's a cappella choir. I asked her how she had discovered her talent. How young was she, for instance, when she realized that her voice had potential?

"Oh, I never had much of a voice," she said.

"What do you mean?"

She explained that although she had always been able to carry a tune, her voice lacked volume and range, strength and gusto. Those qualities just weren't there.

That sounded a great deal like a description of my voice, so naturally I wanted to hear more. "Then how did you learn to sing so well?" I asked.

"I just wanted to so badly that I made up my mind that I would. My dad thought I was crazy and suggested I pursue something I had more natural talent for. And maybe I was a little crazy. Even my singing teacher didn't have much hope. But I continued to take lessons, and I learned how to breathe, and I practiced and I practiced until I got it right. My range gradually increased, and my volume?" She grinned. "Now I don't even need a microphone. I belt it right back to the rear of the hall." Asked to sing frequently, she is not just an adequate singer. Her voice is a megaphone of gorgeous sound.

Although emphasizing the haves rather than the have-nots in our lives probably ought to be the general rule, it is eye-opening to discover what can be done with desire and determination. "I made up my mind I would," she said. And she did.

I was visiting teaching recently when suddenly we heard a shriek from the garage. "What on earth was that?" Molly raced to the garage to see what was wrong. I was relieved to see that she was smiling when she came back. She explained to us that her husband was doing some refinishing. "That was a cry of jubilation, not pain," she assured us. Then she explained that he had been stripping away layers of ugly blue paint that covered some old chairs when he discovered some gorgeous carved wood underneath. "It's a pretty nice surprise."

"I'll say," we agreed.

And it can also be a nice surprise—a shock, in fact—to find strengths through our weaknesses.

Chapter 9

The Essential Talents

Even though he was my "brother" in the group I'd been assigned to in my singles ward, I had trouble feeling comfortable
around Fred. Other group members seemed to feel the same,
for I noticed they avoided him as well. It wasn't that we meant
to be unkind. It was just that we weren't sure how to react to
Fred. He was unpleasant and cynical and rarely spoke without
sarcasm.

Then something amazing happened. Fred began to change.
He smiled more and graciously acknowledged us, eliminating
the snide comments. For the first time he became enjoyable
to converse with. I admit I was a bit distrustful and suspicious
at first. I was sure that the old Fred would be back and that
this was probably just an experiment of some kind. I was sure
that the old Fred, who could cut you to the quick, would be
back soon enough. But at the next outing and then the next,
Fred remained this much more pleasant, even fun-to-be-around
person.

I finally couldn't contain my curiosity any longer. "You're
so different from before," I said after one of our home evenings.
"What prompted you to change?"

Fred seemed pleased that I'd noticed. "It really wasn't anything major," he said. "One day I came home feeling unloved, and I played back the events of the evening. I realized I had no one to blame but myself. I didn't like what I saw. The way I treated others was not in line with the way I wanted to be treated and was not in line with Christ's teachings. I knew I had to make a change."

I let Fred know how much I admired him for his efforts and then I said, "I for one really like the change! You're, well, you're nice."

"Thanks," he answered. "I'm working on it."

Fred must have continued working on it because at a reunion several years later he was still sincerely kind and courteous, still humorous and witty, all in a very pleasant way. I was elated.

Change is a miracle possible to each one of us. It is comforting to know that we can diminish our weaknesses and faults, acquire good habits, and become better each day. Even more comforting is the assurance that though we all came with different talent packages, when it comes to talents essential to our salvation and exaltation—talents of the character and spirit—they are most certainly available to us.

How do we know that? Because our Father in Heaven would not ask us to have those qualities if they were not available to us. Remember what Nephi said: "I will go and do the things which the Lord hath commanded, for I know that the Lord giveth no commandments unto the children of men, save he shall prepare a way for them that they may accomplish the thing which he commanded them." (1 Nephi 3:7).

So even though we may not feel we were born with a great deal of natural shine in some of the qualities we know we need, and even though some of those qualities may not be highly developed in us, we know they are available to us in all their beauty and full glow.

What are these essential qualities? Most of us are pretty much aware of what they are. We know that they deal basically with living a Christlike life: morality, honesty, uprightness, fair-dealing, love and respect for ourselves, others, and our Father in Heaven. Happily, we can all discover within ourselves these resources to be all that we need to be.

Valerie longed for more faith in her life. She recognized that her lack of faith stemmed from relying on worldly knowledge and pride, and she felt bad that she often doubted. She envied those who could say, "I have never had any trouble believing." She wished she too could say fervently, "I know."

One day, Valerie decided to take the necessary steps. She studied, and she found that as she learned more, many of her questions were answered. She also prayed with heartfelt earnestness. Through the Spirit, she recognized some things in her life that she needed to put in order. It took time and effort, but to her delight, faith came. It was always available to her. What joy she felt when she was able to say with certainty, "I really know God lives." How marvelous it felt at last to have that burning she had heard about.

Carol Ann struggled with her habit of feeling critical and judgmental toward others. She recognized that she was often petty and gossipy and that her habit undermined her relationships with neighbors and friends and thwarted her ability to feel close to the Spirit. One day she read in Matthew 7:2, "For with what judgment ye judge, ye shall be judged: and with what measure ye mete, it shall be measured to you again."

Carol Ann didn't think she wanted to be dealt with as harshly as she dealt with others. She prayed fervently for help in overcoming this habit. She made a rule for herself: she wouldn't say anything behind someone's back that she would hesitate to say to the person's face. She decided to try to remember that it was her job to love and understand and leave the judging to our Father in Heaven. If she thought a critical thought, she would immediately try to find something good about that person.

As Carol Ann endeavored to see the good in others, she was amazed to find how wonderfully people treated her and how nice they were becoming. Soon she couldn't believe how great the people in her ward and neighborhood really were. The ability to see good in others was always there for her. How peaceful and close to the Spirit she felt as she was able to let go of her critical thoughts.

Margaret sometimes had a difficult time telling the truth. She knew that her dishonesty stemmed from a desire to have people think well of her. For instance, when someone asked her to do something that her schedule wouldn't permit, Margaret fabricated an excuse that sounded better than the real reason she had. Even when she disagreed with someone, Margaret pretended that she agreed wholeheartedly. When Margaret found herself telling falsehoods to her children one day just because it was more convenient at the moment, she recognized the extent to which telling untruths had become a bad habit in her life.

Margaret decided to take the problem to her Heavenly Father. She prayed for the courage always to tell the truth, even when it was difficult. A comforting feeling enveloped her, and she received the assurance that she had the ability to tell the truth. She decided to keep a chart for herself so that she could record her efforts and be more apt to remember to tell the truth. During the next few weeks Margaret discovered that it is actually easier to tell the truth than to make up lies. She discovered that truth has a much sweeter taste when it flows from the lips. Although she tried to be tactful, she began to look people in the eye when she talked to them. She was elated to sense that people trusted her more. She respected herself more as well, and best of all she felt that the spirit of truth had become her companion and close friend. Finally, after about three weeks, she felt the habit was cemented in her life. The ability to be honest was there for her. It was always there for her.

We can all find the gifts we need to help us when we decide to align ourselves more closely with what the Lord would have us do. I think deep down we know that those gifts are within our reach and that the Lord will help us find them and develop them in our lives. So why is it that we often don't have confidence or faith in ourselves when it comes to spiritual potential?

When a speaker in our sacrament meeting, for instance, asked who felt they would be going to the celestial kingdom, only a few hands went up. Could it be, again, that we feel we have nothing because we have not yet achieved the excellence we think we should already have achieved? Could it be that we feel impatient at our development and think that to be acceptable in God's eyes we must already have all the essential qualities perfectly developed in our lives? After all, Christ did say, "Be ye therefore perfect, even as your Father which is in heaven is perfect." (Matthew 5:48.) We forget that we can't possibly have all such qualities in a perfected state immediately, or even overnight. Although they are there for us, perfection too comes with time and effort.

A neighbor who has overcome an addiction to alcohol and drugs told us in a sacrament meeting how he struggles with feelings of inadequacy, even though he has made great progress, when he sees how far he still has to go to reach perfection. He turns to Doctrine and Covenants 46:9, which tells us that our Father in Heaven blesses those "who live my commandments or *him who seeketh so to do.*" In other words, the direction we are heading in and our desire to reach for those essential talents do count, even if we haven't arrived yet. "Blessed are they which do hunger and thirst after righteousness," one of the Beatitudes reads. (Matthew 5:6.)

This desire and willingness to do something about our imperfections can help us attain what we are seeking, step by step, through patience and love for ourselves and God.

Elder William H. Bennett, in a general conference talk called "Our Goal Is Perfection" (*Ensign*, Nov. 1976, p. 29), quoted part of a poem by Josiah Gilbert Holland:

> Heaven is not reached at a single bound;
> But we build the ladder by which we rise
> From the lowly earth to the vaulted skies,
> And we mount to its summit round by round.

It is also comforting to know that the essential strengths of character are available to us when we are faced with adversity or trials. Although we've been taught that we will never be tried beyond our capability to endure, many of us may secretly feel that there are some things we just wouldn't be able to handle.

I too felt that way. Cancer was one of those trials I knew I would never be faced with because I was sure I just couldn't handle it. Then I found a lump in my breast, and within days I was in the hospital for a biopsy. I soon learned that I did indeed have the disease I had always dreaded. Believe me, I got down on my knees quickly and prayed. I prayed for strength; I prayed for faith; I prayed for all the essential qualities I needed to face this ordeal and to help my family face it as well. To my surprise, the courage and strength and all else required were there for me. I felt Heavenly Father's love in abundance as he let me know that I had the inner resources to handle even this trial because he would make sure they were there for me. I understood more completely the meaning of the Beatitude that reads: "Blessed are they that mourn: for they shall be comforted." (Matthew 5:4.)

But there was something else I needed as well. When life is threatened or we face the possibility that it could be shortened, we find ourselves wanting to know how we are doing. We want an appraisal. I hoped to feel a peace within my heart that I was on target. I yearned for a feeling of sanctification — that I was doing all right in the eyes of my maker. Again, as I prayed, an assurance filled me that though I definitely wasn't perfect, I was doing all right in Heavenly Father's eyes because I was reaching in the right direction and I was doing the best I could. I was trying. And isn't that all any of us can do?

Chapter 10

The Richest Art

"I honestly always thought that the ultimate high would be getting a book published," another writer once told me. "I was sure that that dream come true would be the point of arrival for me—the one success that would suddenly make my life complete."

Having a book in print certainly sounded like my definition of a dream come true. At that moment I was still waiting to hear whether a novella I had been working on had been accepted, and I could think of no greater thrill than walking into a bookstore and seeing on one of the shelves the book I'd worked on so long and hard. Unless, of course, it was having someone actually read that book. For me, right then, a book in print did sound like the success that would complete my life, the X on that mountaintop. I felt that if I had a book in print, I would never ask for anything ever again.

"And sure, it was exciting all right," my friend continued. "It was definitely a thrill. But I've recognized since that real happiness and completeness have nothing whatever to do with having a book in print or reaching any other pinnacle. Real peace and satisfaction come from feeling good about the rest of my life as well, the *whole* of my life—feeling good, for instance, about the job I'm doing with my kids."

"Oh, I know what you mean," I answered, and I did. In fact, I'd recently read a similar insight by Somerset Maugham. After saying that the arts bring much beauty into life, he added that of all the arts, "the richest in beauty is a life well-lived. That is the perfect work of art."

As we talk about talents and gifts, especially the development of some of our individual gifts, I have to say that I've met both men and women who feel unsuccessful or even untalented because they haven't yet achieved what they consider to be eminence or the significant degree of success or excellence they'd had in mind. Yet some of these same individuals are living excellent lives. Living such a life is in and of itself a talent, or as Somerset Maugham called it, an art.

What does the living of such a life entail? Balance comes to mind. We see those who are highly successful in their chosen fields but who neglect to add sheen to other important areas of life. We read of such geniuses as Van Gogh and Mozart who contributed greatly to their arts but who did not seem to have had the happiness of a whole and glowing life.

It's difficult to judge genius, however, because those of us who aren't geniuses can also find it difficult at times to keep life well balanced and to keep ourselves from getting carried away by one narrow aspect of it.

"Gosh, you must really be self-disciplined," a woman once said to me because I wrote. She was implying that I wrote out of sacrifice and was doing something noble. I assured her that my writing had little to do with self-discipline, sacrifice, or nobility but that I wrote out of a need to express myself and share my feelings. Later, as I thought about it, I realized that self-discipline *is* involved. Self-discipline comes in controlling that urgency—in turning off the typewriter and stopping my work when the time I've allocated for writing is up. That can be difficult at times because the inner currents haven't always stopped flowing and all the words I want to say are not yet out on paper. But I know by now that no amount of writing will compensate for my getting carried away and neglecting other aspects of my life.

"I'll bet you'd just love to be able to take off somewhere and have uninterrupted time to write," another friend said to me. I answered yes. That day the dog had the flu, and my laundry room looked like a war zone with unmatched socks threatening a takeover. (Hadn't I just cleaned out that room?)

But then I thought, "Good grief, what on earth would there be to write about? I'd be foolish if I failed to acknowledge that the real joy is not in the writing itself but in my feelings about the things I write—my family members, for whom I wash all these socks, and the humorous, pithy, wonderfully crazy, price- less, and even sacred experiences with family and friends through church activities and through the living of everyday life." And that's why the plug is worth unplugging, even if I'm still anxious to get all those words onto paper.

Happily, I've found that once I do get away from my type- writer, there is satisfaction in those other areas as well. Even cleaning a laundry room can be satisfying when I see order develop out of chaos as I fold the colorful towels into fresh- smelling stacks.

Balance is important to our health and well-being. Some of my friends and I have joked about how we would be perfectly happy to use our bodies as cushions to hold up our heads because we really struggle to obtain the motivation to exercise physically. My walking partner, Pam, and I don't call it working out. We call it working up to getting out. When we do finally get out the door to walk a few blocks, I admit, it feels good. Oh sure, it might hurt a little for a while, but it still feels good. I guess it's the intense self-respect I feel because I actually did it!

Those who have physical abilities may have the opposite problem. They may have more trouble gaining enthusiasm about bobbing those brain cells. Elaine told me about a woman who joined her book club, a woman who admitted she knew that reading was good for her but she wasn't a reader and might have a struggle. Elaine laughed. "She's converted now." Once this woman got a taste of really fine literature through such works as *Les Miserables* and *The Chosen,* she became the proverbial kid in a candy shop. A whole new world had opened up to her. She's struggling, all right. She's struggling to keep this new interest under control.

As we add color and sheen to the whole of our lives, whether it be physical, social, mental, or the essential spiritual, and as we make opportunities for ourselves by getting to know nice people or attending fine plays and musical productions or incorporating in our lives things that are "virtuous, lovely, of good report or praiseworthy," we find our lives enriched.

"We can satisfy ourselves with mediocrity," President Spencer W. Kimball said at one time. "We can be common, ordinary, dull, colorless, or we can so channel our lives to be clean, vibrant, progressive, colorful, and rich." (*The Teachings of Spencer W. Kimball,* ed. Edward L. Kimball [Salt Lake City: Bookcraft, 1982], p. 161.)

When we think of beautiful lives, the word *priorities* also comes to mind. The artist of a beautiful life seems to know what's important. A grandmother who is such an artist told me of a day when she had just cleaned her home thoroughly and was outside working in her yard when her daughter and her family stopped by. "We left the kids in the back for a minute and went into the living room," she said. "In a few minutes these little characters came in, covered in peat moss. They'd apparently been rolling it and throwing it, because it was in their ears, their noses, their hair. The baby had added her ice cream cone to the peat moss on her head."

"Oh, Mom," the daughter moaned. "What shall we do!"

"What do you think?" this wise soul said with a laugh. "Get the camera, of course!"

"But your house!"

"Oh, the house. We'll worry about that later!"

I marveled at her ability to know what matters.

How uptight and worried we often are about details, about having everything just so. How we fret. Just before a particularly hectic Christmas season (I haven't had a peaceful Christmas season yet), when I felt pressure to get the remainder of my gifts purchased, finish my decorating for company I was expecting, get the tree up and ready, and do a trillion other things associated with the season, I thought, "Wait a minute. Does Christ really want me to feel this way about the celebration of his birth?"

I mentioned my uptight feelings to my husband, who didn't seem to understand. Later I sought sympathy from my sister-in-law, knowing another woman would understand. I told her that my husband didn't seem to relate to what I was feeling. "Mine has no idea what we women go through, either, during this season," she said with a laugh. "I think it would be a great idea to just turn over Christmas preparations to the men. They wouldn't worry so much about whether ribbons match paper or whether they have a little something for so and so's cousin's uncle. They'd just skip a lot of details that send us into a frenzy."

"But somebody has to do it," Martha probably thought when her sister remained sitting at Christ's feet while she worked in the kitchen. Uptight, she wanted Mary's help. Jesus' gentle reproval, "Martha, Martha, thou art careful and troubled about many things" (Luke 10:41) could be an injunction to all of us: "Don't worry so much! Don't get uptight about things that really don't matter that much in the eternal scheme of things." As Elder Dallin H. Oaks said, the story of Mary and Martha "reminds every Martha, male and female, that we should not be so occupied with what is routine and temporal that we fail to cherish those opportunities that are unique and spiritual." (*Ensign*, Nov. 1985, p. 61.)

Both Marys and Marthas worry about having too much to do and being unable to get even all the "good" things done. We rush from one thing to another and then worry that we're not doing enough. Just as there are many of us who feel we are not good people because we aren't perfect yet, so there are also many of us who don't think we're living good lives because we aren't doing enough. Recognizing that it's okay to simplify our lives can help, and realizing we needn't do everything at once can ease our feelings of frustration. We also need to accept our limitations and be realistic about what we expect in order to feel at peace with our lives.

A children's book that has always been a favorite at our house contains a series of stories about an owl who isn't very wise. In one episode the owl decides that he really misses his upstairs when he's downstairs, and vice versa. He decides that the solution is to be in both places at once. Rushing upstairs as fast as he can, he calls to himself, only to find he isn't downstairs because he is upstairs. Then he rushes downstairs and calls to himself again, only to discover he isn't upstairs because he is downstairs. The owl finds that no matter how fast he runs, he can't be in both places at once.

I chuckled with my children at the foolishness of this owl, until one day I realized that I often did the same thing. I too expected the physically impossible of myself. Once, when I had a meeting to attend, I got annoyed with myself when I realized I couldn't get there on time and would have to go in after it had begun. But yet, if I had left in time to be at the meeting when it started, I wouldn't have been able to talk for more than a second to an old friend who was having a problem. I would have felt terrible about cutting her off.

Still, in the evenings when all four of my children want

my help urgently at the same time, I find myself feeling guilty and inadequate that I'm not helping all of them all at once. What's the matter with me? I wonder.

Too often I don't stop to realize that I am only one person and can do no more than my best. And each of us is only one imperfect person who has limitations. Heavenly Father is aware of that. At a time when Joseph Smith was struggling, the Lord assured him that he did not need to "run faster or labor more than [he] have strength and means provided." (D&C 10:4.) Knowing that Heavenly Father recognizes that we can only do our best can be comforting. It helps us feel better about ourselves and about the lives we're leading.

Feeling out of control of our lives can also cause us to be frustrated that we aren't doing as well as we ought to be doing. Amy, for instance, had a list to complete but got little of it done. On her way to the bank, she saw a teenage girl who had car trouble, and she gave her a lift home. When Amy got back she realized that her daughter had forgotten her gym clothes, and she rushed to her daughter's school. On the way back from the school, her baby threw up in the car. There went the afternoon, for naturally Amy tended to the baby's needs. The day continued thus, until by its end Amy thought, "I didn't get anything done today!"

In reality, of course, she did get things done. She attended to the most important things, even though they were not on her "to do" list.

It can comfort us to reanalyze our situations and realize that even when we think we aren't getting much done, we may be choosing "the good part" and just haven't recognized our choice. Someone once commented on the "interruptions" that we think prohibit us from getting to the real business of living: "perhaps real life *is* the interruptions."

When we consider our priorities, it would also help to keep in mind that often what the world deems important is of no consequence. When I came home from surgery, my world tipped. I found that many things I had previously thought were terribly important sank right to the bottom, and other things floated immediately to the top, where they belonged.

One acquaintance who is a great artist of life hardly leads what the world would call an exciting life. She isn't concerned much about her appearance and prefers to dress in old levis and thongs. Her kitchen is not decorated like the kitchens in commercials nor is it void of water spots and clutter, but this poem by Ellen P. Allerton could have been written expressly for her:

> Beautiful faces are those that wear—
> It matters little if dark or fair—
> Whole-souled honesty printed there.
>
> Beautiful eyes are those that show,
> Like crystal panes where hearthfires glow,
> Beautiful thoughts that burn below.
>
> Beautiful lips are those whose words
> Leap from the heart like songs of birds,
> Yet whose utterance prudence girds.
>
> Beautiful hands are those that do
> Work that is honest and brave and true,
> Moment by moment the long day through.
>
> Beautiful feet are those that go
> On kindly ministries to and fro,
> Down lowliest ways, if God wills it so.
>
> Beautiful shoulders are those that bear
> Ceaseless burdens of homely care
> With patient grace and daily prayer.
>
> Beautiful lives are those that bless,
> Silent rivers of happiness,
> Whose hidden fountains but few may guess.

("Beautiful Things," in *Best Loved Poems of the American People* [New York City: Doubleday, 1936], p. 127.)

"Beautiful lives are those that bless." That definition could surely fit into our personal dictionaries of comforting thoughts.

Many lovely women don't feel they are living very great lives, and yet they are meeting needs and doing each day what needs to be done. There can be much greatness in small things. Harry Emerson Fosdick said: "To leave the world a bit better, whether by a healthy child, a garden patch, or a redeemed social condition; to know that even one life has breathed easier because you have lived. This is to have succeeded." As we simply meet our obligations with honor, fulfill assignments, do our daily best, we find that we are indeed living successful lives and choosing "the good part."

If we choose to add to the good part, we should recognize the extras for what they are—extras. They are not necessities. Bonnie, an artist of life who lives across the street from me, loves the Christmas season and adds to the good part, or the spiritual aspects, happy memories and great fun as she gets out her Christmas village, bakes up goodies, and displays her beautiful handmade decorations. I believe Bonnie gets even more excited than her grandchildren for their annual Christmas party.

"Do you ever resent having to keep all this up?" I asked her once. She had had surgery that year and simply had to be tired.

"Are you kidding?" she said. "I start looking forward to Christmas in June and would celebrate it all year if I could. I love the season!"

Childlike joy can help us not only to develop and learn but also to look at life as the wonderful adventure that it is. We can learn to see each day as a Christmas package that we can open with excitement. Or we could look at life as a treasure hunt. If we live with wonder and excitement, we aren't afraid to try new things. Consequently we find more interests, strengths, and, yes, talents, at the same time we are finding more pleasure in our day-to-day living.

Chapter 11

The Greatest Talent

Generally when we hear success stories about athletes, we hear of winners who overcame great odds or who kept trying. It's uplifting to hear about those who wouldn't give up. But when my neighbor Doug told about his old high school friend, a fellow track runner named "Squeaky" Jensen, I recognized a different kind of winner.

Come to think of it, Doug never mentioned how many track events Squeaky won. He only said that even if Squeaky had had his own event that day, he'd still have been there to cheer for Doug.

And his cheering style was delightful. First Squeaky would cheer for Doug at the starting point, "Go, Doug!" But Squeaky wouldn't stay put, as the other spectators did. No, when Doug turned at the loop, Squeaky would hightail it straight across the center of the field so that when Doug came around to the other side of the track, his "soul" supporter would be there again, cheering for him, reassuring him, calling to him. In fact, each time Doug came around the loop Squeaky would be there, "Go for it! You can do it! Keep it up. You're doing great!"

"And when I was heading for the finish line on that final

lap," said Doug, "when my lungs were in my throat and my feet felt like slabs of cement, when I was beginning to think maybe I really didn't need to win just this once, then I'd hear Squeaky's voice again, cheering for me above all the others: 'Now, Doug! This is it! You're a winner!'

"To this day," said Doug quietly, "I still don't know whether my wins were due to my talent in track and field or to the great talent a buddy had for cheering."

The ability to feel joy at others' gifts and abilities and to sincerely want the success and development of others is not often thought of as a talent, but surely it is one of the most important and essential of talents. It isn't always easy, however, to be thoroughly thrilled at others' successes.

When a friend told of her sister-in-law's stunning scrap-books, she added, "She's so artistic it's sickening." The rest of us laughed because I'm afraid we understood. Sensing such feelings in others, however, can discourage us from developing our own talents and strengths because we want to keep our friends, too.

Yet, it can feel threatening to us when someone else seems to be progressing faster than we are or is achieving success in something we're weak in. I remember the night I was asked to speak at a seminar about the book I'd written that had finally been printed. I admit I was feeling a bit giddy and a little amazed at being there. Then the hostess pulled me aside to meet another writer (someone she knew I'd be *thrilled* to meet) who had five books in print. Frankly, I wasn't thrilled to meet that other writer right then. I knew as I said, "Well, isn't that nice," that the words sounded less than sincere, because they were.

In my estimation, it is easier for us to be compassionate when others stumble or have hardships than it is for us to be excited when they take steps in their development and do well — especially, let's face it, if they do *really* well. Too often we feel life is the race, and we're all in competition.

That's why it surprised me and then inspired me when almost everyone I interviewed for this book mentioned others who had helped them recognize gifts in themselves and had encouraged them to develop those gifts. I soon concluded that the "rare" gift of rejoicing in the successes of others isn't so rare after all. It was encouraging to discover that there are many "Squeaky" Jensens out there.

Some mentioned teachers who were willing to help them develop their gifts and to share their knowledge unselfishly. Francis Urry said that the same teacher with whom he'd had a bad start in his audition sensed his intense desire to develop his dramatic skills. She was willing to overlook Francis's pompous, old-fashioned style and help him learn what he needed to learn. I heard emotion and even reverence in his voice as he spoke of her.

Peter Lassig said that the head gardener on Temple Square who had been his first boss taught and nurtured him. The head gardener saw to it that Peter got the right education, even though Peter was a perfect stranger and small for his age when he announced in his job interview, "I want to take over your job — well, someday."

Others mentioned family members who cared. One poet I spoke with told of a sister who claimed she had no talents of her own but said, "I'm thrilled with the talent you have, and I'm so proud of your accomplishments."

"No talents?" said this poet. "My sister's unselfish willingness to appreciate, inspire, and encourage is a great gift. Without her I'm not sure I would ever have had the courage to develop my ability."

Where would any of us be if there were no one to appreciate us?

A surprising number spoke simply of friends or acquain-

tances who backed them up and believed in them. Often it
was the combined good-will of many along the way. One writer
told me that she had been ready to quit trying because she'd
had some set-backs when the words of a stranger encouraged
her to keep writing. "How could she have known, unless it
was through the Spirit, the words that would inspire me once
again?"

We have probably all had in our lives those who encouraged us or cheered for us to develop in the *essential* talents,
and we bless their names. Sometimes ward members or neighbors or friends gave us the encouragement we needed. Our
bishop spoke of an elderly brother in his home ward who
always took the time to acknowledge him and shake his hand.
"Let's see how that old missionary handshake is coming along,"
he'd say.

Even now, when I go back to the ward where I grew up,
I look for a particular sister who always pulled me aside to
fuss over me. She thought I was great, and consequently I felt
great when I was around her. Even as adults, we know the
power of those who take the time to joke with us or who simply
acknowledge our existence with a smile or friendly hello. I
know I'm not alone in having to admit that there have been
times when the anticipation of seeing certain bright faces of
those real Saints was the only reason I got out of bed in the
morning and made it to church.

The ability to feel sincere joy at others' gifts and development is not only a gift that many have developed but it is
also a gift we can all develop.

How can we do that?

We can quit competing. Competition is futile not only because we have different materials to work with but because it
is contrary to our purpose on this earth. Carol Lynn Pearson
expressed that idea beautifully in this poem:

God does not grade
On the curve,
I'm sure of it.

But we sit around
Like high school students
In an important class,
Whose teacher has drawn
On the blackboard
The tiny wedges
For the A's and the E's.
And the great bulge
For the C's.

We sigh in veiled relief
As the person down the row
Messes up,
Because it makes us
Look better
And probably means an E
For him, which is good,
Because while we have
Nothing against him personally
It means an A is more
Available to us.

And we secretly sorrow
When the person in front of us
Does really well,
Although we like her okay,
Because there goes another good grade,
Darn it, and we're looking
Worse and worse
And slipping further down the curve.

And God, I think,
Sits at the front of the class,
Holding A's enough for all,
Watching us
Work out our salvation
In fear and competition.

("The Grade," in *The Widening View* [Salt Lake City: Bookcraft, 1983], pp. 58–59. Used by permission.)

The Savior taught us in the parable of the talents that all of us are potential winners. One servant developed four talents, another multiplied his to ten, and yet no comparisons were made between the two servants who had developed their respective gifts. Only the servant who hadn't tried to develop his talent was chastised. By looking at the broader picture, we can quickly see that others' gifts and skills actually benefit us. Their development affects our communities, our lives, and our world in real ways. Where would we be if we didn't have others to help us?

As we help each other magnify and multiply gifts, we better all our lives. And by working together, we can get so much more done in building the kingdom. But how do we get to that level where we want others to succeed and develop—not for us but for them and for a common purpose?

Isn't it love that helps us reach that higher plateau? "Charity suffereth long, and is kind," the scripture says. "Charity envieth not; charity vaunteth not itself, is not puffed up, doth not behave itself unseemly, seeketh not her own, is not easily provoked, thinketh no evil . . . And now abideth faith, hope, charity, these three; but the greatest of these is charity." (1 Corinthians 13: 4–5, 13.)

If charity is that desirable in our Heavenly Father's eyes, then he will definitely help us develop it in our own lives.

With that charity, we can find it easier to want the successes of others so much that we encourage them to succeed. With charity, we accept the uniqueness that others are entitled to, even if their gifts are different from others. We allow people to be themselves and don't expect them to be exactly like us.

When I mentioned my problem with unmatched socks to a neighbor who visited my home, she said she could not recall ever having lost a sock. She wasn't necessarily trying to appear superior — she was merely stating a fact. Nevertheless, her statement upset me. Never lost a sock! What was the matter with her? This woman was not from this planet! I decided I didn't want to associate with her anymore. Then I thought, wait a minute. The Spirit whispered *charity,* and I realized that she had every right to be different from me. If she had a talent for management, I should feel joy for her and encourage her, not expect her to be any less than she is for my sake. Maybe she could even give me a few pointers!

When we accept differences and let others know that we appreciate them in their uniqueness, we also encourage them to develop in their best ways and all ways. We encourage growth by accepting differences. Abraham Lincoln was referring to his stepmother when he said, "All that I am or ever hope to be, I owe to my angel mother." She took his part when his father thought reading was a waste of time and education frivolous. She also defended Abe's sense of humor. Once, when he was chuckling about something nobody else understood, she said, "Abe is entitled to his own jokes."

And aren't we all entitled to our own differences?

Uncritical love provides us with the desire to grow. With charity, we find it is so much easier to look for the potential in others and not the faults. I remember well the day my boss called me into her office many years ago. I had made some pretty stupid blunders that first month on the job, and I was terrified. What if I got fired? I desperately needed this job to get through school.

But instead of chastising me for the errors I had made, this woman patted me on the back. "Hey, you're doing superbly out there," she said. "You're a real ace at that typewriter."

"But I've had some major goof-ups."

"You're trying hard, and that's the important thing. Mistakes are a part of the training program."

Then this kind and lovely lady proceeded to mention some

of the things I'd done *right*. I might as well have sprouted wings, the way I floated out of her office. After that I worked even harder to be the employee she'd said I was. The boss was cheering for me!

I try to remember that woman now as I help my children. How easy it is to notice the wrong notes they hit when they practice playing the piano, for instance. I try to help them correct those wrong notes, sure, but I also try to remember, for pete's sake, all those right notes they're hitting as well.

It's so much easier to see faults, isn't it? They ping out at us and strike an unpleasant chord. But how much more we all benefit from hearing praise and encouragement. I suspect one word of encouragement is equivalent to about fourteen thousand words of criticism when it comes to the motivation to improve that they instill.

Words! What impact they have. It made me cry when a stake leader told us about her first day in high school. Tall and gangly, she lacked confidence and hadn't yet discovered her own self-worth. She anticipated rejection for herself, but her greater concern was for her older brother. He had worked hard to become a student body officer and a "somebody" in the school. What a comedown she felt it would be for him to acknowledge her as his younger sister. Some of her friends' brothers had asked them to please refrain from speaking to them in the halls — and they were girls who were not even half bad, according to Carolyn.

Though her brother hadn't made such a request and she knew he never would, she made up her mind. She would not put her brother in a position where he would need to ac-knowledge her. She would avoid him at all costs and wouldn't mention to anyone that they were related.

The first day of school had barely begun when Carolyn, searching for a class, discovered herself in the front hall directly in front of the prestigious central stairs where a group of the "big men" of the school congregated. There among them was her brother. Quickly Carolyn ducked (which is difficult to do when you're six feet, two inches tall). She started around the stairs, but it was too late. Her brother had spotted her.

And what did this young man do? He called out his sister's name clearly and insisted she come closer. "Then," Carolyn said with tears in her eyes, "My brother put his arm around me and pulled me toward the group. With all sincerity, he said gently and lovingly and with pride, 'This is my neat sister, Carolyn.'

Carolyn sniffed. "Neat? Believe me, I wasn't *neat* in the way we used the term back then. But that my brother thought I was and was even willing to say so in front of his friends made a big difference in my high school experience."

Each of us has an Elder Brother, who set the example for charity and who can help us attain charity in our lives. Charity is Christlike and of him. Charity doesn't require much time. It just emanates. Others sense good will. They know when we are cheering for them just by the looks on our faces. Love radiates.

When we give lessons or talks, don't we seek out the faces that are smiling encouragement? Can't we tell who wants our successes and who is cheering?

I remember myself as a mixed-up adolescent pouring out my feelings to my mother. I realize now that she couldn't have understood what I was trying to say. I still don't understand those feelings, even now. But as she listened attentively, I could see by her face how hard she was trying to understand and how much she cared. She didn't know what to say to help me, but she helped me just the same.

We sense that kind of uncritical love when we find it in our neighborhoods, in our wards, even in strangers we meet. When I saw an old friend I hadn't seen for quite a number of years at the supermarket, we eagerly asked about each other's lives. After she told me about her job, I hesitated to tell her about my writing because I'd learned by now that some old friends didn't seem excited about it. Yet, realizing that if she should hear anything later, she might think it a bit peculiar that I hadn't mentioned anything when I'd been given the chance, so I told her I'd been doing some work with my typewriter. Marsha immediately quizzed me for details. I blurted out that I'd written a book and that it was in that very store. She raced for the book section, hauling me along with her. She grabbed my book and eagerly glanced through it. With sincere jubilation she gave me a hug that nearly knocked me over. "I'm so proud of you!" she said. "I didn't know you were so talented."

Talented? I knew who was talented in the most essential and loveliest of ways.

Happily, feelings of appreciation are contagious. Later that night a sister in the ward called to ask my opinion about a story idea she had—an idea I recognized instantly as a good one, one that would help others and that was both fresh and clever—but I had always had trouble supporting this woman. My feelings, to be honest, had always been: "You can already bake sweet rolls, sing, sew, and paint. Good grief, do you have to do this too?"

Okay, there it was, that competitive fear. But now, as I remembered Marsha's sincere and complete happiness for me, my need to compete dissolved. Instead, another feeling, one of sweet peace and love, was taking its place. As I said the words, "I think you might have a real winner here, and I hope you'll go with it," I meant them. Believe me, it felt good to feel that way.

I discovered as well that helping others does not hinder our own progress. But if we think about it, that only makes sense. If there is a replenishing when we give in ordinary ways, how can there not be an even better replenishing when we give in the best ways?

We've talked about inventorying and helping ourselves "see" all that we have. It's even easier when we do it together. We encourage love to grow in our families when we conscientiously share things we appreciate about each other. We encourage greater feelings of sisterhood when we help neighbors, friends, or just acquaintances discover their gifts or develop gifts they already know about.

The other night, I read again the parable of the talents. What a different outcome that story of the three servants would have had if one of those servants had had the talent of a character from one of Christ's other parables: the good Samaritan. Remember that helpful and loving soul who showed such concern for a fellow traveler? He was a man with a talent not so different from that of Doug's friend, Carolyn's brother, my amazing friend Marsha, and many others. I was pretty sure that if *he* had spotted his colleague burying his allotment, he would not have stood by. Nor do I think he would have harbored any secret feelings of gladness at his friend's blunder. He wouldn't have thought to himself, "Oh good, he's bungling it. All the better for me. Now I'll look even better when our lord returns."

On the contrary, I think the good Samaritan would have rushed to his friend's side. "Wait! What are you doing? Oh, please don't bury your talent. It's far too precious to bury."

And when his brother expressed his feelings of inadequacy or his fear of the master, I believe that that loving servant would have consoled him with the words, "Oh, but you don't need to feel that way. There's nothing to be afraid of. You've been given this talent because our lord believes in you. He loves you and wants you to succeed, and so do I."

And when at last some hope flickered in the eyes of this fearful and reluctant servant, I believe the good Samaritan of encouragement and good-will would have put his arm around his brother and prodding him gently would have said, "Come with me. I'll help you understand the ways of the merchants. Don't be afraid. We'll multiply our talents together."

When we help each other, we do exactly that. We multiply our talents together, supporting each other, caring about each other, wanting the best for one another. Surely that is the way of the Father, and that is why, if we have charity, it is easier to be there for others. We become anxious to cross the field to cheer on our friend. We want to reach out and boost one another towards the highest and finest that is within us. We want to reinforce all that is good and excellent in each other for the benefit of all and to our Savior's honor. Surely that ability is one of the most Christlike abilities we can attain.

Within each of us is the power to love at this level. It's a talent that's available to us, one that we can develop at the same time we're developing in a myriad of other ways. When we develop that talent, the light it reflects will glow as did the Star that shone many years ago. Like that star, the talent of charity represents, as it emulates, our Savior.

Yes, each one of us is talented. We have treasuries of glorious riches, more magnificent than we can comprehend. Many of those treasures are right before our eyes.

I believe our Father in Heaven wants us to recognize and appreciate our talents and possibilities and acknowledge them. I believe he wants us to cherish ourselves and esteem our worth as beautiful and individual creations and recognize the full spectrum of gifts he has given each of us. I'm convinced that we don't need to win or even place in any kind of a talent race to be important in his eyes or to win a place in his kingdom. But as we see more clearly who we are and all that we have, we can progress with joy and confidence in our own personal race to heights that will eventually amaze us.

As we encourage ourselves and others and feel of Heavenly Father's spirit, I believe we will at last be able to say without reservation, "Yes, I am talented. Heavenly Father has blessed me with some wonderful gifts and he will help me use those gifts to benefit his children. With his help, I'll go to work!"

Index